Elements of
Project Management:
Plan, Schedule, and Control

Elements of Project Management:
Plan, Schedule, and Control

M. Spinner

Prentice-Hall, Inc., Englewood Cliffs, New Jersey 07632

Library of Congress Cataloging in Publication Data

Spinner, M.
  Elements of project management.

  Includes index.
    1. Industrial project management. I. Title.
HD69.P75S68   658.4'04   80-25470
ISBN 0-13-269852-8

To that individual whose unequaled
zeal for knowledge provided the inspiration
and encouragement for this endeavor.

Printed in the United States of America

10 9 8 7 6 5 4 3 2

Editorial/production supervision
  and interior design by Leslie I. Nadell
Manufacturing buyers: Joyce Levatino
  and Gordon Osbourne

Prentice-Hall International, Inc., *London*
Prentice-Hall of Australia Pty. Limited, *Sydney*
Prentice-Hall of Canada, Ltd., *Toronto*
Prentice-Hall of India Private Limited, *New Delhi*
Prentice-Hall of Japan, Inc., *Tokyo*
Prentice-Hall of Southeast Asia Pte. Ltd., *Singapore*
Whitehall Books Limited, *Wellington, New Zealand*

About the Author

M. (Pete) Spinner is Manager, Plant Engineering Department, Glass Division, Ford Motor Company, and a part time Lecturer in project management principles. In the latter capacity, he is presently conducting classes at the Lawrence Institute of Technology in the associate studies program. He has also taught at Oakland University, Henry Ford Community College, and the University of Tennessee.

He was employed by several engineering and construction firms before entering Ford Motor Company. At the present time he is in a responsible managerial position involving the planning and scheduling of major new buildings and facilities as well as expansion programs. In this capacity, he has also provided strategic and operational plans and schedules for proposed facilities in Europe and Mexico.

Mr. Spinner is a graduate in Civil Engineering from the University of Pittsburgh and completed his graduate work at Harvard University, earning a Master of Science degree in Civil Engineering. While on a tour of duty with the U.S. Army, he attended selected engineering classes in Army Specialized Training Programs at Purdue University.

Contents

Preface

A few years after I began applying network planning with other project management principles in my work as an engineering and planning manager, I entertained the thought of documenting my experiences at some appropriate time. This text is my initial effort in realizing my goal.

Supplementing my experiences in this text are the research and the lecture material that I use for teaching my project management classes.

The text is written so that readers of varying backgrounds in education and experience can understand its contents. In addition to the basic fundamentals, the text includes expansion of project management methods that will be useful to those with previous training and experience.

The reader, who may be our future planner, will be shown the principles (or "tools") to arrange an effective plan and schedule, and after the project has started, the methods to control the direction of the project to its successful completion. All of these phases are presented in the sequence of how an actual project evolves, and a sample project is used as an illustration for applying the project management techniques throughout the discussion in the text.

The text is arranged in such a manner as to illustrate first, the basic fundamentals of organized planning and scheduling; second, monitoring and controlling projects (with emphasis on such communication styles as status reports); third, handling of project costs and labor allocation; and finally, computer application. There are also two chapters devoted to a companion network planning method, Project Evaluation and Review Technique (PERT). This approach to project management implementation may be beneficial in some areas of business and industry, and of special note are the time and cost status reports illustrated in these sections.

When calculations are required, elementary arithmetic supplemented with simple graphs is used. Purposely avoided are any detail analytical exercises that may be used for substantiating the derivation of several of these techniques. Using successful applications as examples can show more than any management science displays such as linear programming or mathematical modelling.

The text emphasizes that the planning and scheduling can be done and is accomplished without a computer; however, there are situations where the application can make good use of a computer. One chapter explains how the speed and accuracy of computers is especially useful for large and complex programs.

Included in the text are problems concerning the major subjects that can be used for those readers who want to determine how well they understand the elements of project management. Several sample projects are included that can be selected for a term project problem. These problems are so designed as to incorporate all of the aspects of project management that are covered in this text. Completed project problems are useful as reference material.

Most of the actual applications shown in the text are from my experiences at Ford Motor Company. This is "where it all started" for me in applying and developing the techniques explained in this text.

I wish to acknowledge Ford Motor Company for their permission to use portions of a Ford training manual entitled, "Training Course 3315 — Critical Path Method." I also want to state that Ford Motor Company is not responsible for the accuracy or content of any of the material used for inclusion in the textbook. The contents are of my own design and I assume full responsibility.

I wish to express my appreciation to those who shared in the preparation of this book: Chairman Wayne H. Buell, President Richard E. Marburger, and Dean Richard E. Michel of the Lawrence Institute of Technology, for their support and cooperation; my son, David, and my cousin, Nina Mayers, for their proofreading efforts; Nan Scullin for her untiring efforts in preparing the initial diagrams and cover design; and a very special thanks to Louanne Snyder, my

"Girl Friday" on this project for her valuable suggestions and particularly for having the patience and ability to transfer my handwriting into a typed manuscript.

M. (Pete) Spinner
Southfield, Michigan

1

Introduction

A knowledgeable authority in project management has stated: "The requirements for project management are simple — you only need infinite patience, understanding, and wisdom."[1]

There is much truth in this statement, especially in the handling of modern-day projects that are complex and are of large proportions. However, there are tools available, simple to learn and apply, that can alleviate the problems encountered in project management. Among these tools are the following:

1. Planning, scheduling, and controlling time and costs.

2. Program reporting and forecasting time duration.

3. Cost reporting and forecasting total expenditures.

4. Use of computers, in conjunction with the above, especially for large and complex projects.

We shall list several definitions before proceeding with a discussion of the major topics.

Project management in the business and industry fields is defined as managing and directing time, material, personnel, and costs to

---

[1] Eric Jennett, "Guidelines for Successful Project Management," *Chemical Engineering*, July 9, 1973.

complete a particular project in an orderly, economical manner; and to meet established objectives in time, dollars, and technical results.

One can define a *project* by means of the following distinguishing characteristics:

1. There is a specific start and a specific end point.

2. There is a well-defined objective.

3. The endeavor is unique and not repetitious.

4. The project usually contains costs and time schedules to produce a specified product or result.

5. A project cuts across many organizational and functional lines.

Project management principles are disciplines employed in planning, scheduling, and controlling a project. The most popular, *network planning*, is a relatively new technique used to help accomplish the successful practice of project management. There are other techniques that complement the application *network planning* and are included in the discussion of this text.

- Management by objectives
- Management by exception
- Cost analysis
- Labor allocation/leveling

The use of these principles is associated with careful, detailed planning; therefore, the user is forced to think through the project.

NETWORK PLANNING

The most widely used project management principle is network planning. This technique is used to plan, schedule, and control a project consisting of a group of interrelated jobs (which may also be called work items or activities) directed toward a common goal. The network planning method is especially useful for those projects that have a well-defined starting point and a well-defined objective; project performance is usually very good when using this method. Modified versions of the usual network planning methods are required to plan and schedule production control or process control operations or any type of activity that involves continual scheduling on a continuous flow of activities.

History of Network Planning

The initial undertaking in planning a project is the development of a graphical diagram. The idea of using diagrams to plot the progress of a project is quite old. Things that look like network diagrams appear in the literature as early as 1850. In particular, George Boole, who worked in the field of logic and algebra, used diagrams to explain propositions in logic and the flow of logical problems. The Prussians in the late nineteenth century developed diagrams to show tactical movements on battlefields. They showed where their troops would be, where the enemy troops would be, and how a battle would progress. One of the favorite pastimes of military people is still the construction of diagrams to show how famous battles occurred.

Another use of diagrams arose from the work of economists. An article published in 1944 indicates that economists developed arrow diagrams designed to show the flow of systems and the interrelation between systems. The diagrams look surprisingly like those used in network planning or some of the other systems that we have today.

The need for improved planning and progress evaluation techniques to help control the utilization of manpower, material, and facilities became apparent at approximately the same time in the 1950s. The pioneering application of the network diagram and the *critical path concept* was a jointly sponsored venture of E. I du Pont de Nemours and Company and the Sperry-Rand Corporation. The objective of this venture was to improve the planning, scheduling, and coordination of du Pont's engineering projects. By September 1957 an actual application was conducted on a pilot system using the UNIVAC I computer, and from this initial effort, network planning and the critical path method evolved.

Simultaneously, the Navy was devising a system to plan and coordinate the work of nearly 3,000 contractors and agencies on the Polaris missile program. From the Polaris project came the *Program Evaluation and Review Technique* (PERT), which is credited with helping advance Polaris development by at least two years.

Today many industries use networks to plan projects of varying size and complexity. Procurement and installation of tooling, building facilities, and machinery are being scheduled under network control. Network planning has many other applications. It can be used to plan design operations, construction projects, administrative programs, maintenance operations, model changeovers, and practically any other series of actions that, when combined, form a complete program having a start and a finish.

The multitude of different names applied to network diagramming methods, such as CPM (Critical Path Method), PERT (Project Evaluation and Review Technique), PEP (Project Evaluation Procedure), and LESS (Least Cost Estimating and Scheduling), merely distinguish the application techniques. The most commonly used are CPM and PERT. The main distinguishing characteristic is that CPM traditionally has been considered activity-oriented, whereas PERT is event-oriented. However, these differences are gradually melting away, and the term "network planning" is now commonly used as a general term to describe all these types of operational programming.

The network diagramming procedure used in this text is the *Critical Path Method* (CPM), which requires that all jobs be completed with no allowance for failure. This can limit the use of CPM in such programs as planning research projects, feasibility studies, test programs, and preparation of proposals. Such projects will have situations where there are alternative approaches, and all of the "paths" may not only have an unpredictable outcome, but all but one may be aborted.[2]

Graphical Evaluation and Review Technique (GERT) is a network diagram system that allows for jobs to be started when there is uncertainty as to whether the preceding jobs may or may not be completed. (However, for GERT to be effective, one of the jobs needs to be completed.)[3]

The reader is advised to gain a more thorough knowledge of the CPM technique before attempting application of GERT.

In network planning, the terms *planning* and *scheduling* are not synonymous. By definition, a plan is a proposed method of action or procedure. Planning may or may not be dependent on timing. Planning indicates *what* activities are to be accomplished.

Scheduling is the development of a timetable that puts time estimates next to the plan and indicates *when* activities are to be accomplished.

Bar Charts

The traditional approach to planning and scheduling has been through the use of *bar charts*, which portray the timing and duration of each activity in a project. These charts are familiar to almost everyone in industry. Basically, they depict graphically the jobs to

---

[2] Jerome D. Weist and Ferdinand K. Levy, *A Management Guide to PERT/CPM: with GERT/PDM/DCPM and Other Networks*, 2nd ed., © 1977, p. 150. Adapted by permission of Prentice-Hall, Inc., Englewood Cliffs, N.J.
[3] *Ibid.*

be done and the timing for each job, as shown in Figure 1-1. This type of bar graph indicates the beginning and end dates for each of Jobs A, B, C, and D. These jobs represent the engineering, material procurement, construction, equipment delivery and installation phases, respectively, of an engineering project. In many cases, we might find that one or more of these jobs is subdivided and detailed on a second chart. To illustrate, Job A might be divided into several major components, each of which would become a bar or a bar graph.

A chart of this kind provides some valuable information, but essential data are missing. From the standpoint of effectively planning, scheduling, and controlling a project, additional and more accurate information is required. For example, the relationships among engineering, procurement, construction, and equipment delivery and installation (activities represented by Jobs A, B, C, and D) cannot be shown and the following questions cannot be answered:

1. What parts of these jobs can be performed concurrently?

2. What parts of each job are necessary to be completed before other parts begin?

3. Must certain jobs or parts of jobs be given priority in order not to hold up completion of the project on schedule?

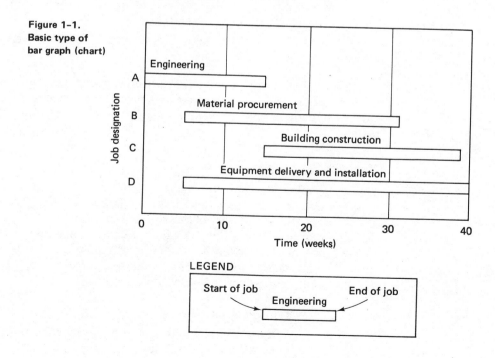

Figure 1-1.
Basic type of
bar graph (chart)

4. Do some jobs or parts of jobs have optional starting and end dates, and what specifically are these optional dates?

Henry L. Gantt, one of the pioneers in scientific management, developed many kinds of charts and records for planning purposes. About 40 years ago, Gantt developed connected bar charts which bear some resemblance to arrow diagrams. Different kinds of shadings have been incorporated in bar graphs to show the activities that could be started early; however, there are limitations. Revisions to these charts are difficult to make and require a great deal of time to update, especially as projects have grown in size and complexity.

Using basically the same project elements as shown for the bar graph, a simplified *network diagram* can be illustrated graphically, as shown in Figure 1-2. Network diagrams overcome the deficiencies of bar chart construction by providing essential information necessary in planning projects:

1. Network diagrams explicitly show interrelations between jobs.
2. A network diagram shows which jobs can be done concurrently, which ones precede, and which ones follow other jobs.
3. Jobs with critical schedules are specified with their required beginning and completion dates.
4. Jobs of a noncritical nature are also shown with optional beginning and end dates.

Although bar charts have limitations for planning purposes, they have been refined over the years to provide an excellent communication expedient to management by summarizing the status of projects.

Network Planning Procedure

Planning, scheduling, and controlling projects, the three phases in the project management cycle, are handled separately for more effective results in the network planning procedure.

The planning phase can be the most time consuming of the total project process: however, the time spent planning can also be the most rewarding. Planning is determining *what* work is to be done.

Planning a project will follow these steps:

Step 1. *Establish Objectives*

a. State objectives that will be derived from the requirements which motivated the project.

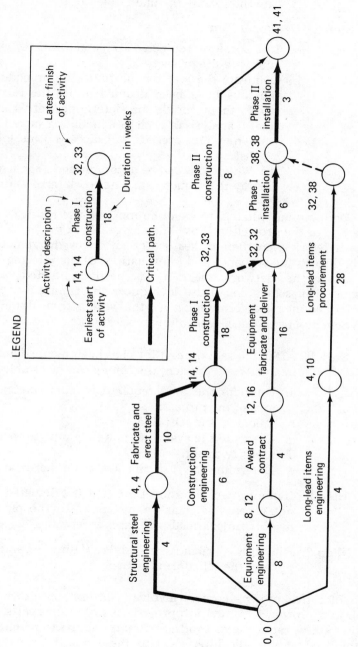

Figure 1-2. Network diagram

   b. List interim objectives or milestones that are significant in meeting the main objectives.

Step 2. *Develop a Plan*

   a. List the jobs (or activities) that have to be done to complete the project.
   b. Delineate the jobs by the following procedure: After the jobs have been decided upon, the relations between them should be determined. This involves a careful analysis of each job, including such items as:
      (1) Which jobs precede and succeed other jobs on the list.
      (2) Which jobs can be accomplished concurrently.
   c. Portray the sequence in a network (arrow) diagram.

Determining what is to be done must be the result of a careful analysis of the project by those knowledgeable in the particular field. The network plan then makes use of an arrow diagram to graphically display the sequence and interrelations of the jobs required.

After the network diagram has been completed, scheduling begins. The scheduling phase introduces the timing aspects of the job. Scheduling is determining *when* the work is to be done.

Scheduling a project will follow these steps:

Step 1. After the sequence of jobs has been planned and laid out in a network diagram, the timing can be established.

   a. Estimate the time required to complete each of the jobs in the project.
   b. Calculate the schedule.
   c. Compute the available time to complete each job.
   d. Identify the critical jobs.
   e. Determine the float times of the noncritical jobs.

Step 2. If the project duration time that is calculated initially is not acceptable, make adjustments to the plan so as to meet a project deadline that is acceptable.

Step 3. Establish a calendar schedule. (Using a bar chart may portray the schedule effectively.)

Effective project control involves constant monitoring of each job in the project. Actual job progress is noted on charts or various other status reporting methods. Summary reports to management are submitted at periodic intervals, and these reports can be prepared weekly, biweekly, or monthly, depending upon the dynamics and scope of the project. The reports will project completion status (generally including costs) and will highlight critical items that may jeopardize the schedule.

Supplementing the network planning technique as the major "tool" in managing a project to a successful completion are such techniques as management by objectives; management by exception; cost analysis, including time/cost trade-offs (or cost minimizing); and resource allocation. Next, we define these techniques as they apply to project management.

MANAGEMENT BY OBJECTIVES

Once the goals have been identified, an orderly procedure can be set up so that all of the combined efforts are directed in such a way that the goals are achieved. Through network planning, application of *management by objectives* can be readily achieved:

1. Because you have a goal, you know whether or not you are on the right road.
2. You can assess results all along the course of the project.
3. By regularly assessing performance of your goals, you know when you are "drifting."
4. You will perform with maximum effectiveness by knowing what goals the project requires and how well you are going in relation to these goals.

MANAGEMENT BY EXCEPTION
(Recognizing Problem Areas)

Network planning facilitates application of the management by exception principle by readily identifying the critical operations. The critical operations usually make up about 20% of the project activities that can affect the overall progress. Through network planning there is a clear definition of just how far each of the other jobs can slip behind schedule without affecting overall progress. This permits true *management by exception*, since management can concentrate on the critical jobs. At the same time, limits are set up for the remaining jobs that must be met if the project is to be completed on schedule. Any slippage beyond these limits immediately signals the need for management attention.

COST ANALYSIS

Network planning also makes it possible to consider costs in the same way that project timing aspects are handled. Cost scheduling is helpful to those funding the project. It is a valuable tool for projecting cash flows and for preparing a planned expenditure distribution. On large projects cost schedules prepared in a disciplined manner are the basis of determining property taxes and depreciation schedules.

There are cost disciplines designed to ensure that project spending is contained within approved or authorized amounts. One effective project cost control technique used is the *indicated cost outcome*. It provides a periodic review and evaluation of the spending status of open projects to determine if spending is in line with approved authorizations. Specifically, an indicated cost outcome procedure will provide an "early warning system" for potential project overspending or underspending. Planning future spending levels and comparing them with authorized amounts will determine whether anticipated project spending may require additional authorization.

The results of the planning phase should produce the least costly schedule for a feasible project duration. The *minimum-cost expediting technique* available through the use of the network planning procedure does just that. It produces schedules for a number of different project durations, each of these being the minimum-cost schedule for that particular project duration.

How can the project be rescheduled to meet the required deadline at minimum additional cost? The first step in shortening the duration of a project is to select the critical jobs that can be reduced. We will assume that unreasonable time estimates have already been identified and eliminated. A reduction in time can usually be made through expediting overtime, assignment of additional people, use of air freight, and so on, but at some additional cost to the project.

Next, the additional cost involved in reducing project duration is matched with the benefits that can be realized when the time of the project is reduced. The objective is to reduce the duration of those jobs that can be shortened with least additional cost.

For this purpose, a cost-minimizing program has been developed as a management discipline. Through this discipline, rescheduling, including the selection of jobs to be accelerated, is accomplished in such a way that whether the final cost is smaller, larger, or unchanged, the added cost has been minimized.

LABOR ALLOCATION/LEVELING

In the initial phases of network analysis, there is no restriction on the availability of labor. However, an important problem in labor allocation is that only so many persons are available to perform the work in a project. Another problem in personnel scheduling is to make efficient use of the labor that is available. It is necessary to avoid labor-usage curves that show sharp peaks and valleys for a number of reasons:

1. Efficient use of labor will cut costs.
2. Effective use of labor will reduce unnecessary overtime.
3. A reputation for offering life-of-the-project employment will make it easier to attract and hold the best skilled labor.

All sorts of intuitive methods for leveling the use of workers have been tried. The intuition that enabled the practitioners of these methods to enjoy partial success also told them that purely intuitive methods were woefully inadequate. When intuitive methods are supported by a disciplined approach to resource allocation, quite satisfactory results can be obtained.

APPLICATIONS IN BUSINESS AND INDUSTRY

The use of network analysis with the associated project management principles for project administration has become popular in industry, business, and government. The use of project management principles is growing because they aid in satisfying a need to assist in resolving the problems encountered from the ever-increasing complexities in modern-day projects.

Construction Industry

Because the work conditions that make up a construction project are dynamic in nature and changes are commonplace, network planning has become very popular in this industry. Arrow diagramming has become standard practice for planning and scheduling construction projects.

Changing conditions, such as fluctuating labor and design changes, are the rule rather than the exception in a typical construction project. Where alternative plans are constantly being evaluated, project management principles are the tools used to successfully complete projects. Rigid disciplines are needed to keep the programs on schedule within budgeted amounts.

Industrial Projects

As industrial expansion is closely allied to construction operations, the use of network planning in all facets of business activity, including industrial expansion, has been most productive. Marketing objectives, financing methods, facility evaluations, and so on, are laid out with alternative plans and made available for review by management at all levels. The logic and timing developed from arrow diagrams serve as reliable supporting data in feasibility studies and business planning presentations.

Marketing Programs

Planning a marketing program can involve the efforts of many diverse individuals in research and development, engineering, manufacturing operations, sales, and various management groups. These personnel, all of whom have an interest in the program, are essential to successfully market a product. A marketing program may begin with an extensive market analysis survey of potential consumers and continue through the construction of a new manufacturing plant, possibly in a foreign country. The inclusion of an advertising campaign adds to the complexity of the project. To plan such a program requires a great deal of coordination of the participating activities.

In recent years, marketing groups have adopted the network analysis approach in planning marketing programs. A network plan will clearly show all the essential steps in conducting the program, and it will also define the responsibilities of the participating groups. The coordinating requirements are also made visible, so that no group can overlook its relationship to others.

As this important business segment involves a spectrum of diverse activities, the first sample problem used in the text is a marketing project. The project is titled "A New Product Introduction" and it illustrates many project management techniques. As the sample problem will illustrate, the marketing project need not be long or too detailed to be effective. What is important is the ability of the method to provide an adequate plan. The arrow diagramming approach accomplishes this for this particular program.

Hospital Capital Programs

Delays so commonly experienced in hospital projects have been avoided by network planning, which is diagrammed from the beginning, the predesign phase, to the end, the occupancy phase. The technique has helped to create positive management interest early in the program. Hospital officials, in recognizing problems early, have avoided months of "drifting," so prevalent in hospital programs that have used unrealistic planning methods.

Government Activities

For almost 20 years network planning diagrams have been included in the specifications prepared for proposals submitted for governmental activities, including the United States Navy, the United States Army, the United States Air Force, the Department of Defense, and the National Aeronautic and Space Agency.

The major reason for using network diagramming is that governmental agencies require so much service and approval that documentation of their activities is a necessity. Network diagramming lends itself to these demands and its utility has extended beyond this purpose to allow it to be used in other areas. In addition to its use in construction projects and planning programs, network planning diagrams are being used for administrative plans.

Computer Application

Using a computer to apply the technique of network analysis for large projects is essential. A computer saves substantial time in determining which jobs must be given priority (those on the critical path), in making schedule changes, in leveling the use of workers, and in accomplishing a variety of other planning, scheduling, and control functions. Chapter 7 is devoted entirely to use of the computer in project management applications.

ADVANTAGES IN APPLYING PROJECT MANAGEMENT PRINCIPLES

Today's planner can use project management techniques to guide and control the course of a project with more confidence than by use of any of the older methods. However, these techniques cannot and will not replace the value judgments of human beings. The results are only as good as the effort that is put into them.

To be a useful tool, a network must reflect reality as closely as possible and be continuously revised to keep it accurate. Above all, for the utmost effectiveness, complete backing by top management is essential. They must understand and accept the method if it is to be used successfully. With effort, participation, and cooperation, the advantages are many. Following are some of the more important benefits that will be gained by its use:

1. It makes participants think through a project in greater detail.

2. It enables more efficient use of resources, such as personnel, equipment, space, and money.

3. It gives a clear picture of the project that is readily communicable to everyone involved, including new personnel.

4. It enables true management by exception. Management can react quickly to the critical items that may jeopardize a project.

5. It enables real control of projects that previously may have been too unwieldy for anyone to understand.

6. It provides management with data on which to base plans for minimizing investment costs or maximizing return on investment.

7. It enables quick rescheduling of a project to meet changing or unpredictable conditions.

8. It can help improve labor relations.

9. It is a proven system for planning, scheduling, and controlling projects.

10. It provides a graphic picture of the work by showing the proper relationships among the project work items.

2

CPM/Project Planning

Planning is a vital management function; in fact, most management authorities consider planning to be the most important function. Yet, the responsibility of developing plans is often superseded by such items as "troubleshooting" or reviewing ongoing jobs or operations. Although these tasks are important, they cannot replace the time that needs to be allotted for the planning phase.

The quality of planning is also an important consideration in the successful outcome of a project. After experiencing a trying project, one manager surmised: "Possibly the reason that the plan failed was that there may not have been a plan at all."

Providing a good technique for planning a project is the purpose of this chapter.

There are three phases in the project management cycle; planning, scheduling, and control. In planning, we determine *what* has to be done in accomplishing a project, establishing the sequence of work, and specifying the interrelations between jobs. Timing, or *when* the work is to be done, is not generally considered during the planning phase. In more detail, the planning phase follows this procedural outline:

Step 1. *Establish Objectives*

    a. Objectives are normally established by higher management and/or dictated by a particular company goal.

      b. Interim objectives or milestones may also be specified.

Step 2. *Develop a Plan*

      a. Prepare a list of jobs required for the project.
      b. Determine the relationships between the jobs:
        (1) What jobs precede a given job on the list?
        (2) What jobs follow a given job on the list?
        (3) What jobs can be accomplished at the same time?
      c. Portray these relationships in an arrow diagram.

In the next phase, scheduling, we are concerned with the timing aspects, that is, how much time each job is expected to require for completion, and when each job will be scheduled to begin and end.

People familiar with the work required must provide the information as to what is to be done, the sequence to be followed, and the time required to complete each job.

For complex projects, the computer is used to make the critical path timing calculations accurately and rapidly. The use of the computer is most helpful in the third phase, project control, for providing timely follow-up information in a convenient and effective form, and to update and adjust the scheduling data quickly as the job progresses. Providing reports on the current status of the project is an important communication link.

To summarize, planning, scheduling, and control of a project will follow this sequence:

1. *Project Planning*

    a. Objectives.
    b. Content of project.
    c. Arrow diagram.

2. *Project Scheduling*

    a. Time estimates.
    b. Timing calculations.
    c. Job scheduling.

3. *Project Control*

    a. Follow-up.
    b. Updating.
    c. Reporting.

Drawing the arrow diagram is a part of the planning phase, and should be done initially without reference to the timing aspects. Separating planning and scheduling helps to simplify their accomplishments, and should result in a more effective job being done in both areas.

THE ARROW DIAGRAM

As the final part of the planning phase, the arrow diagram shows the sequence of jobs to be accomplished and their interrelations. The arrow diagram provides several important advantages:

- A disciplined basis for planning a project.
- A clear picture of the scope of the project that can be easily read and understood by someone who is not familiar with the project.
- A means of communicating what is to be done in the project to other people involved, some of whom are not familiar with its details.
- A vehicle for use in evaluating alternative strategies and objectives.
- A means of defining interconnections among jobs and pinpointing how the responsibilities for accomplishing the jobs fit into the total project.
- Assistance in refining the design of the project.
- An excellent vehicle for training project personnel.

After project personnel have carefully analyzed the project, determined what jobs must be performed, and outlined the flow of work to be followed, they translate the results into an arrow diagram. An arrow is drawn for each job. The sequence of the arrows indicates the flow of work from the beginning of the project to the end. The diagram has one beginning point and one end point. Arrow junctions are called nodes. They are usually numbered, which is useful for identifying the location of arrows in the network.

Arrows

In an arrow diagram, an arrow is used to represent a *job* or *activity*.

- The work is assumed to flow in the direction in which the arrow points.

- The job, therefore, begins at the left end of the arrow and finishes at the right end (at the head of the arrow).

- The arrows are not time-scaled.

- Job sequences are indicated by the way the arrows are interconnected. In the following illustrations, the arrow interconnections show job sequences:

Job A must be completed before Job B is started.

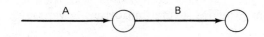

Job A can be done concurrently with Job B.

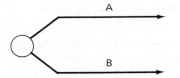

Jobs A and B can be done concurrently and must be completed before Job C begins.

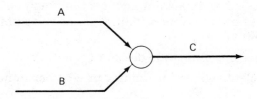

Two types of arrows are used in diagramming:

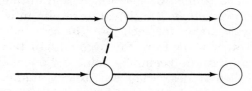

1. Solid arrows represent jobs or activities.

2. Dashed or dummy arrows show special interrelations.

The solid arrow has several features:

1. It represents a job or activity that consumes time (has a duration) and resources.

2. Work is assumed to flow in the direction in which the arrow points.

3. The length can vary (time or duration is not indicated by the length).

There is no simple answer to the question: How much work should be grouped under a job? A job may represent work of considerable complexity or a small detail of the total project, depending on the purpose of the network.

In a network designed for management use, each arrow would represent a major activity of the project. The diagram would include only major elements, thus providing an overall view of the entire project.

On the other hand, if the network will be used by persons who will supervise or perform the work, each arrow should represent a small segment of the project. Often, both a general diagram, consisting of major elements only, and a detailed diagram will be prepared for a project.

Nodes

In network diagramming, the beginning and end of each arrow is called a *node* or an *event*. A node or event is a point in time and has no duration. For convenience of notation, an arrow is sometimes said to go from i to j. The i represents the beginning of the arrow; the j represents the end of the arrow. An arrow is uniquely identified by its i and j; for example, "Arrow 2,3" is the "B" activity in the following illustration:

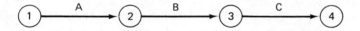

- The circles with numbers 1, 2, 3, and 4 are nodes.
- Each arrow (job or activity) is identified by two nodes — the i node at the beginning of the arrow and the j node at the end.
- Job A is identified as Job 1,2; Job B as Job 2,3; and so on.

Work Sequence

The arrow diagram must indicate the *sequence* in which the work will be performed according to a plan. Since some variation in work sequence in a project is often possible, it should be noted that *every arrow diagram represents someone's specific plan* for accomplishing the project. As the plan changes, so must the diagram.

Three questions are used as guides in arranging the sequence for each job:

1. What precedes the job?

2. What follows it?

3. Which job(s) can be performed concurrently with it?

A review of some of the basic points involved in developing an effective diagram is provided later in the chapter in the sample problem, "A New Product Introduction."

Effective planning of the jobs or activities in a project require that certain techniques need to be adhered to in diagramming the network. Several of the points to be considered when diagramming are shown in the following illustration:

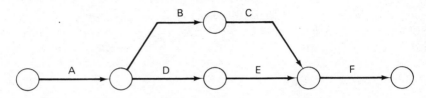

- The position of Job B in the illustration:
  a. Job B follows Job A.
  b. Job B precedes Job C.
  c. Job B can be performed concurrently with Jobs D and E.

- Jobs C and E must be completed before Job F can begin.

- Jobs B and D may start as soon as Job A is completed.

- When two or more arrows begin at the same node, this does not mean that the work they represent will be scheduled to start at the same time. For example, Jobs B and D may start as soon as Job A is completed; however, their scheduled starting times depend on how much "float" each job has.

- Two or more arrows that end at the same node do not necessarily have an identical "finish date." Both Jobs C and E must be completed before Job F can begin, but one might finish before the other.

- If Job H can start after half of Job G is completed, Job G should be divided into two parts: G1 and G2.

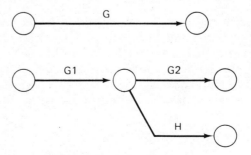

- PERMITTED

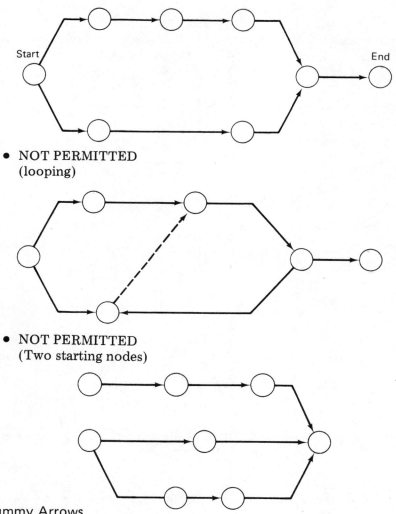

- NOT PERMITTED
  (looping)

- NOT PERMITTED
  (Two starting nodes)

Dummy Arrows

In an arrow diagram, *dummy arrows* express relations between jobs
that are not indicated by solid arrows. The dummy arrows are used
as restraints and as a convenience in drawing the network. A dummy
arrow can be used to maintain the node identification.

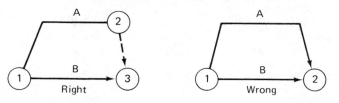

Dummy arrows are drawn as dashed lines and, if possible, are placed at the end of an activity.

Dummy arrows do not represent a job or activity; they have no duration and do not consume resources, such as labor, dollars, and so on. The principal uses of dummy arrows can be illustrated as follows:

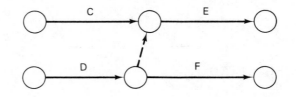

1. • Jobs C and D must be completed before Job E can begin.

   • Job F can be started as soon as Job D is completed.

   The following diagram would not properly represent these relations:

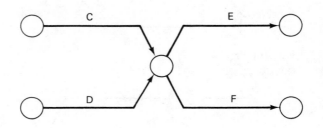

   • Job F is overstrained. This diagram shows that F must follow C and D, whereas F is required only to follow D.

2. The dummy arrow may also be used for convenience or to save time in drawing the diagram. To illustrate, assume that a diagram has been drawn which has over 100 activities. An activity (Job M) occurs near the bottom of the network and must be followed by an activity (Job J) that occurs near the top of the network. Instead of redrawing the network so that Jobs M and J could be shown with solid arrows, which would require considerable extra work, a dummy arrow is drawn from Job M to Job J.

3. Another use of the dummy arrow is to identify arrows uniquely — to avoid duplicating a set of node numbers when identifying different arrows. This situation is illustrated in the following diagrams:

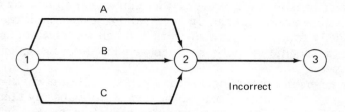

Since "Job 1,2" could refer to any one of three jobs, ambiguous identification results. This situation is called *branching*. Computer programs, which use node numbers for identification, would not be able to process the network data properly. In the following diagram each arrow has a unique node number:

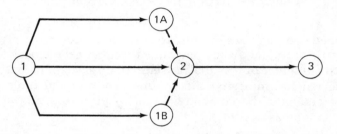

In general, nodes should be numbered in such a way that each job has a unique identification and can be located easily in the network. Beyond this, each computer program for processing project management networks may have its own special node number requirements. Only a few typical requirements will be discussed here.

Some older computer programs require that nodes be numbered consecutively in ascending order; the integers "1, 2, 3, . . ." are used and each arrow flows from a lesser integer to a greater integer. However, very few current computer programs require consecutive numbers. Some current programs still require that arrows be numbered with ascending integers, but they do not require that consecutive numbers be used. Consecutive numbering could cause a problem when the network is subject to continual updating requiring new arrows to be added and some existing ones to be eliminated.

To avoid this, a numbering sequence with gaps between integers is often used: for example, "1, 5, 10, 15, ..." As arrows are added later, unused node numbers may be assigned from the proper interval to maintain an ascending sequence.

More recent programs contain sequencing routines within them, thus eliminating the ascending-order requirements. These programs generally will accept either numeric or alphabetic node designations or both. It should be noted, however, that it is easier to visually follow the flow of work through the diagram and to locate a specific activity if some general ordering scheme is employed.

The person numbering a diagram should inquire whether the computer program to be used subsequently contains any numbering restrictions. The new product introduction project will be used to illustrate the planning process.

DEVELOPMENT OF A NETWORK DIAGRAM: A NEW PRODUCT INTRODUCTION

An established company has decided to add a new product to its line. It will buy the product from a manufacturing concern, package it, and sell it to a number of distributors selected on a geographical basis. Market research has indicated the volume expected and the size of sales force required. The company wants to place the product on the market as soon as possible.

1. *Establish Objectives*

Introduce the company's new product as rapidly as possible.

2. *Establish the Jobs Required*

The first step in developing the diagram is to establish the jobs required for accomplishing the project. Generally, the list of job descriptions is developed by personnel experienced in the type of work involved. (See Figure 2-1.)

Proper listing of every step required to accomplish the project is of great importance. It is vital that all phases of work be encompassed by the jobs listed. Any omissions will cause inaccuracies in scheduling and may result in failure to complete the project on time.

A job description list should be made which lists the major phases of work involved in a project. After the jobs have been decided upon, the relations between them should be determined. This involves an analysis of each job.

There are several basic tasks that must be performed during the development of an arrow diagram. The procedure followed in accomplishing these tasks may vary with the individual. For example, one diagrammer may obtain the list of jobs for the project and then jot down the relations between jobs before

ACTIVITIES IN THE PROJECT

The following activities are to be planned along with the relations among them:

1. Organize the sales office: Hire the sales manager.

2. Hire sales personnel: The sales manager will recruit and hire the salespeople needed.

3. Train sales personnel: Train the salespeople hired to sell the product to the distributors.

4. Select advertising agency: The sales manager will select the agency best suited to promote the new product.

5. Plan advertising campaign: The sales office and the advertising agency will jointly plan the advertising campaign to introduce the product to the public.

6. Conduct advertising campaign: The advertising agency will conduct a "watch for" campaign for potential customers.

7. Design package: Design the package most likely to "sell".

8. Set up packaging facility: Prepare to package the products when they are received from the manufacturer.

9. Package initial stocks: Package stocks received from the manufacturer.

10. Order stock from manufacturer: Order the stock needed from the manufacturer. The time given includes the lead time for delivery.

11. Select distributors: The sales manager will select the distributors whom the salespeople will contact to make sales.

12. Sell to distributors: Take orders from the distributors for the new product, with delivery promised for the introduction date. If orders exceed stock, assign stock on a quota basis.

13. Ship stock to distributors: Ship the packaged stock to the distributors in accord with their orders or quota.

Figure 2-1. Activities required for a "New Product Introduction"

beginning the network; another individual might go from the job list right into the diagramming and develop the job relations as he or she proceeds through a series of rough and final diagrams.

The basic tasks to be performed include listing the tasks required to complete the project, dividing the tasks into groups representing major sections of the project, determining the relations between the tasks, and drawing the arrow diagram.

3. *Divide the Jobs into Groups Representing Major Sections of Work*

As an initial aid to establishing the relations between jobs, the project may be divided into groups of closely related functions under the categories of work to be performed.

In the example, the jobs have been grouped under the major headings "Stock," "Packaging," "Sales," "Distributors," and

"Advertising." These logical groupings simplify the task of determining how the jobs relate to each other. (See Figure 2–2.)

The groups can be established in this example through simple logic. In a complicated project, the diagrammer must be familiar with the details of the project or obtain assistance from experts. The experts would not only define the major categories, but would establish the relations between jobs.

4. *Determine Relations between Jobs*

The basic relations between jobs proceed from the planning assumptions made by the project planner. Note that these are preliminary plans at this point. Additional information will be obtained as the plan is refined. After the data are set up, someone knowledgeable would review the data.

Establishing job relations for a project generally involves a substantial amount of discussion regarding how activities oc-

MAJOR SECTIONS OF WORK

Stock
Packaging
Sales
Distributors
Advertising

Stock

Order stock
Package stock
Ship stock to distributors

Packaging

Design package
Set up packaging facility

Sales

Organize sales office
Hire sales personnel
Train sales personnel

Distributors

Select distributors
Sell to distributors

Advertising

Select advertising agency
Plan advertising campaign
Conduct advertising campaign

**Figure 2–2.
Groups representing major sections of work**

curring in different departments should be connected in the diagram. The resulting agreement on the flow of work should promote understanding of how various efforts and responsibilities tie together in the overall project.

5. *Draw Subdiagrams*

While the relations between jobs are being determined, it may be helpful to draw a subdiagram (Figure 2–3) for each group of jobs. Another way may be to determine the relations between jobs before starting on the subdiagrams. A combination of both schemes may also be useful for this step. When the subdiagrams have been developed, they are combined to form a complete diagram.

6. *Draw Complete Diagram(s)*

The last step in diagramming the project is to draw the complete network. This may involve:

- Drawing a preliminary diagram.
- Making necessary revisions to assure that the job relations are shown properly with no overrestrictions and "looping," "branching," and so on.

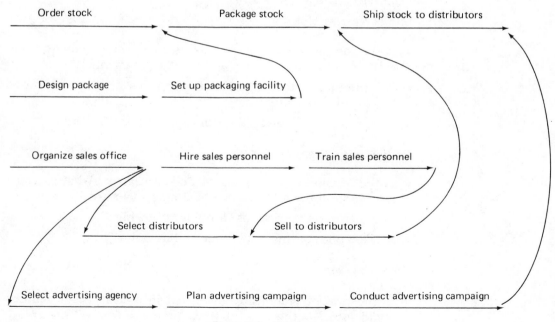

Figure 2–3. Subdiagram

- Drawing a final diagram that provides a clear graphic display (Figure 2-4).
- Checking the final diagram for accuracy and effectiveness.

It is possible that several preliminary diagrams will be drawn before the final diagram is completed. One preliminary diagram would ordinarily suffice, but projects containing input of several activities may represent different stages of network development. However, a second diagram emphasizes the idea that two people diagramming the same project will formulate different patterns and can produce equivalent results from the same jobs and job relations.

Different planners might also establish different plans, and that will be reflected in their diagrams.

Arrow diagramming is a critical part of the planning phase of a project management cycle. Although the diagram will be only as good as the plans of those who developed it, it is an excellent technique. It may also be considered as a device for improving the plans by laying out the plan in clear and unambiguous detail. In this manner, planning assumptions and decisions are subjected to the test of logic.

Planning Diagram Check List

List of job descriptions:

- Is the job detail suitable for the user (top management, other management, professional, and technical personnel)?
- Are the jobs stated as basic functions that can be understood by the intended audience?
- Does the list include all the work required for the project?

Preliminary Diagram(s)

- Is the relation of each job specified accurately? What precedes it? What follows it? What can be done concurrently?
- Are there overrestrictions? looping? branching?
- Is there one starting point? one ending point?

Final Diagram

- Is the project graphically displayed in a clear, easy-to-understand form? Is the flow of work simple to follow? Are groups of closely related jobs easy to identify?

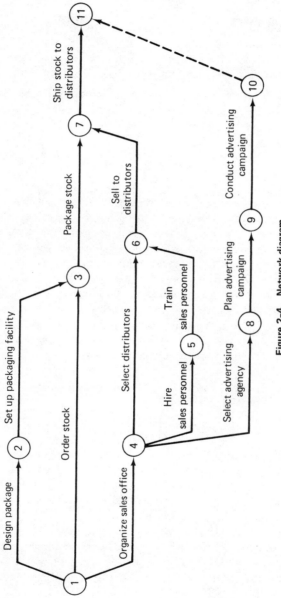

Figure 2-4. Network diagram

- Is the network properly identified? Does each pair of numbers apply to only one arrow? Is the numbering scheme consistent with the computer program to be used?

The final questions relate to the complete planning diagram. Will the network serve:

- As an adequate base for the initial scheduling of the project?
- As an effective communication medium for evaluating, establishing, and controlling the project?

SUMMARY

Planning is the most important step in the project management process. Translating the jobs (and their sequence) into a graphical diagram (or a network) needs the most time. It is very common to hear someone respond, "I always do this in my head," upon being approached with the network analysis technique for planning; however, complexities of current projects dispel that approach. A disciplined analysis for planning a project is essential.

Modern business methods can no longer rely on hunch and intuition as the basis of decision making. However, this technique does not replace good judgment but, rather, relies on good judgment to be an effective management tool.

Planning starts with having a complete understanding of the objectives. Then the following steps need to be taken:

1. Predetermine all of the activities or jobs that must be done to complete a project.

2. Determine the sequence in which the jobs are to be done.

Finally, the development of an arrow diagram consists of preparing a list of the jobs required for the project, determining the relations between the jobs, and recording these relations on an arrow diagram. If all these steps are performed skillfully, the diagram will furnish a valuable planning tool to the personnel involved in implementing a project.

A graphic analysis provides a picture of the scope of the project. With this picture, there exists a vehicle for evaluating alternative strategies and objectives, a means of defining the interrelationships among jobs, and an excellent device for instructing personnel in the details of a project.

3

CPM / Project Scheduling

As stated previously, there is a planning phase and a scheduling phase in network planning. The planning phase, which was covered in Chapter 2, involves the use of the arrow diagram for analytical purposes. The purpose of this section is to describe how a project can be scheduled once the planning cycle is completed.

The first step in scheduling is to obtain time estimates for each job in the project. It is vital that the time estimates obtained be realistic in order to produce a good schedule for meeting deadlines and avoiding unnecessary project costs.

After the time estimates are obtained, the timing calculations begin. Optional starting and finishing times for the work items are developed as well as determining the critical work activities. This information is the forerunner of a complete schedule, making possible more effective use of personnel, eliminating unnecessary overtime, scheduling scarce equipment for maximum utilization, and possibly most important, controlling the cost of the project within its planned budget.

TIME ESTIMATES

A time estimate is obtained for each job in the project immediately after completing the initial arrow diagram. It may be accomplished before completing the planning phase, because at that point adjustments can be made to the diagram, if necessary, to meet management objectives. The time estimates may also be modified after the project begins. Usually, this becomes necessary if there is a delay in the work that will extend the duration of the project or if work is progressing more rapidly than was indicated by the original estimates.

The network diagram normally uses a single time for each job. The time estimate, usually determined by an experienced person, is the amount of time that the job will require under a specified set of conditions. The conditions may be as follows:

- Normal: The usual amount of labor, equipment, and so on, will be used.
- Expedited: Might involve the use of one or more factors such as overtime, extra personnel, and additional equipment. The result is added cost.

First Estimates (Planning Stage)

The first estimates are made on the basis of how much time the job should actually take if everything proceeds on a normal basis. Persons familiar with the work to be performed should make the time estimates based on their best judgment. As network planning involves as accurate detail as possible, it is necessary to avoid any tendency toward "padding" the estimate to provide a "cushion" for contingencies, or underestimating because of undue optimism.

When the initial time estimates have been established, they are added to the arrow diagram. (See Figure 3–1.)

There are certain rules to follow in applying the estimates on the diagram:

- Place time estimates on the bottom side of the arrow.

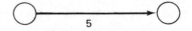

- Show time units with each arrow.

- Use whole numbers.
  a. Manual calculations to develop schedules require whole numbers.
  b. Most computer programs using the critical path technique for calculating schedules require whole numbers. (However,

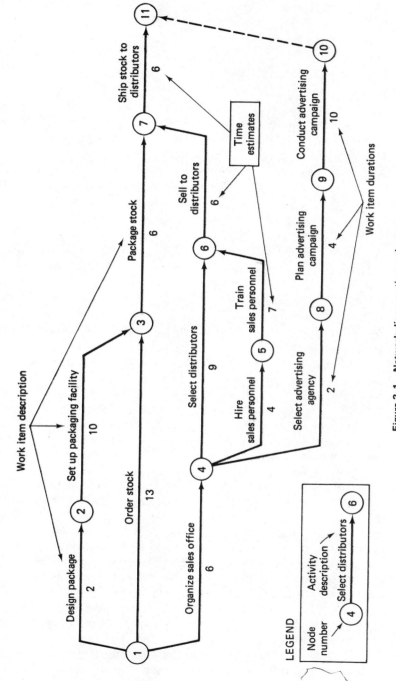

Figure 3-1. Network diagram: time estimates

33

there are diagramming techniques, such as PERT, in which decimals are accepted.)

Second Estimates (Planning Stage — If Project Duration Must Be Reduced)

When the estimated duration of the project has been determined, it is examined relative to prior objectives. If the project duration, assuming "normal" conditions, is not satisfactory, new estimates must be made for some jobs. The method for determining the initial duration and which jobs must be shortened is related to the critical path technique for calculating the schedule and will be discussed later.

Third Estimates (Changes Occurring on Critical Path)

As work progresses on the project, some of the jobs may be completed before or after the scheduled time. If these changes are on the critical path and affect the project duration, modifications in the time estimates and the schedule will be required. When critical path jobs are finished ahead of schedule, it may be desirable to reschedule succeeding jobs so that an advantage can be gained by reducing the project duration.

If jobs on the critical path are not completed on schedule, adjustments must be made in time estimates and the schedule to assure that the project will be completed within the scheduled project deadline.

Persons familiar with the project who are supplying the estimates may be influenced by previous experiences, creating a bias in their estimates. To offset this bias, a method using three time estimates can be adopted.

The three time estimates — optimistic, most likely, and pessimistic — for each activity are used to offset the bias that may be present in one time estimate. The range of the time estimates also gives some indication of the scheduling risk involved; for example, a wide spread between the estimates shows considerable uncertainty about the time actually required to accomplish an activity.

Most Likely Time (or Normal Time): The first time estimate requested is the most likely time. It is the time that would be most frequently required if the activity were repeated many times under similar conditions. It is also the normal job time estimate that would be shown on the arrow diagram.

Optimistic Time: The shortest possible time required for completing an activity is the optimistic time. Here it is assumed that everything goes as planned: deliveries of material occur on schedule,

CHAPTER 3 / CPM/PROJECT SCHEDULING

machines operate without major breakdowns, personnel perform work within work standards, and the like.

Pessimistic Time: The maximum possible time required to complete an activity is termed the pessimistic time. This is the time required for doing something if just about everything goes wrong: in short, the worst possible situation, including delays, accidents, equipment delivery difficulties, bad weather, and so on.

From these three pieces of information, an expected time is derived for the project with this formula:

$$\text{Expected time} = \frac{(\text{Optimistic time}) + 4(\text{Normal time}) + (\text{Pessimistic time})}{6}$$

This formula represents a weighted average of these three estimated times with two-thirds of the weight given to the normal time, one-sixth to the pessimistic, and one-sixth to the optimistic.

Those experienced in using the three estimates have found that the expected time will be biased toward the pessimistic time. As the one-estimate approach usually has a contingency built in, it will usually provide about the same estimated value as the three-estimate approach. One provides a good check for the other.

MANUAL TIMING CALCULATIONS

After time estimates are obtained, the timing calculations can be made. For a small project, these calculations are usually performed manually. We will use a sample problem (the planning diagram shown in Figure 3-1) to illustrate how to perform manual calculations. The time estimates are shown on the diagram. The problem consists of determining the earliest start times, latest finish times, and total float for a product introduction project.

Earliest Start Time

The term *earliest start time* at a node means the earliest time that any job can be started from that node. Jobs that begin at Node 1 are assumed to start at Time 0. For a given job, the earliest start time can be determined by adding the time estimate for the preceding job to the earliest start time for the preceding job. (See page 37.)

The time elapsed between Time 0 and the earliest start time at a node thus represents the shortest period of time that will permit the completion of all preceding jobs that lead into that node.

Guides

The following guidelines should be considered when calculating the earliest start times for a project:

- The calculation of earliest start times commences with Node 1, the beginning of the arrow diagram (Time 0), and continues through each node to the end of the diagram.

- If only one arrow leads into a node, the earliest start time for jobs starting at the node is determined by adding the earliest start time for the preceding job to the time estimate for the preceding job (note Node 8):

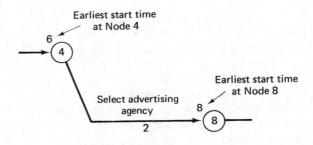

- If more than one arrow leads into a node, the earliest start time calculation is made through each of the arrows. The largest total is the earliest start time for the node, as noted at Node 7:

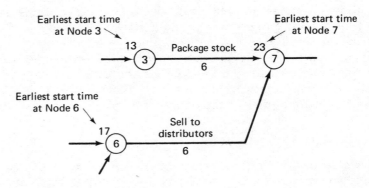

Application

Several representative calculations of earliest start times for the product introduction project are as follows:

Earliest Start Time

Node 1 The earliest start time at Node 1 is set as time 0.   0

Node 2 Design Package requires 2 weeks. The earliest start time for Node 2 is, therefore:

0	Earliest start time at Node 1
+2	Time estimate for Job 1,2
2	Earliest start time at Node 2

2

Node 3 Two arrows lead into this node:

Set Up Packaging Facility requires 10 weeks: $2 + 10 = 12$

Order Stock requires 13 weeks: $0 + 13 = 13$

The larger total is used.   13

Node 4 Organize Sales Office requires 6 weeks.

0	Earliest start time at Node 1
+6	Time estimate for Job 1,4
6	Earliest start time at Node 4

6

By using the same approach to calculate earliest start times for the remaining nodes, the earliest start times for all nodes are calculated and are noted in Figure 3-2.

Project Duration

At this point it can be seen that the jobs on the longest path in the diagram (the critical path) total 29 weeks for completion. This is the minimum project duration for this particular plan with these time estimates.

Latest Finish Time

The term *latest finish time* is the latest time that a job leading to a node can be completed without lengthening the duration of the project. The latest finish time is required in identifying the activities on the critical path and in calculating float for jobs in the network. (See pages 42, 43.)

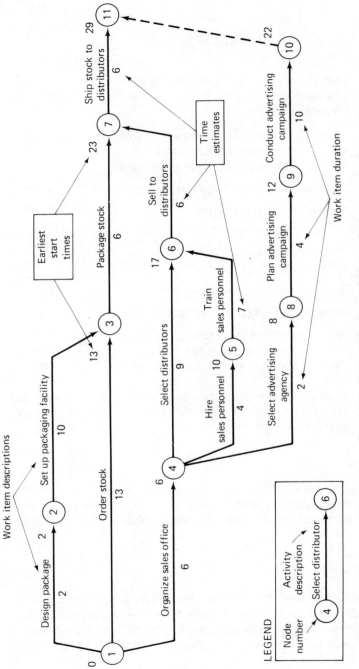

Figure 3-2. Network diagram: earliest start time

38

Guides

The following guidelines should be applied in determining the latest finish times for a project:

- The project duration must first be determined by calculating the early start times.

- The calculation of latest finish times involves working from the end node back through each node to the first node in the project. The project duration is the latest finish time for the last job.

- If the duration for a project is 29 weeks and Job 7,11, which requires 6 weeks, is the last job in the project, the latest finish time for jobs coming into Node 7 is 23.

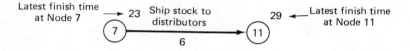

The latest finish time for Node 7 is determined by subtracting the Job 7,11 time estimate from the project duration (the latest finish time at Node 11).

29	Latest finish time at Node 11
− 6	Time estimate for Job 7,11
23	Latest finish time at Node 7

If more than one arrow originates at a node, the calculation of latest finish time is made via each arrow and the *smallest* result is used.

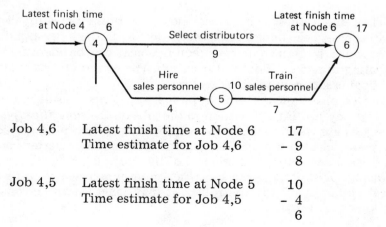

Job 4,6	Latest finish time at Node 6	17
	Time estimate for Job 4,6	− 9
		8
Job 4,5	Latest finish time at Node 5	10
	Time estimate for Job 4,5	− 4
		6

The latest finish time at Node 4 is 6 days, the smaller of the two results. Were the latest finish time for jobs coming into Node 4 set at 8 days, there would not be enough time remaining to complete Job 4,5 by its required latest finish time of 10.

Application

Several representative calculations of the latest finish times for the new product introduction project are as follows:

		Latest Finish Time
Node 11	The latest finish time for the end node is the project duration.	29
Node 10	Job 10,11 (Dummy) is 0-day duration.	
29	Latest finish time for Node 11	
– 0	Time estimate for Job 10,11 (Dummy)	
29	Latest finish time for Node 10	29
Node 9	Job 9,10 requires 10 days	
	$29 - 10 = 19$	19

Calculate the remaining latest finish times in the same manner. The latest finish times for all nodes in the project are noted in Figure 3–3.

When the earliest start times and latest finish times of all the activities have been determined, the critical path, the longest path on the network in terms of time requirements, can be identified by calculating the "total float" of each job. The method for calculating total float is shown in the next section.

The emphasis on the critical path may, at first, result in a tendency to pay too little attention to the jobs on the *subcritical paths*. These jobs are also important to the project, and their progress along each path must be monitored with the same degree of attention as the critical items during the progress of the project.

Delays, or slippage, on a subcritical item may cause it to be the critical path, and if not controlled, it may lengthen the estimated duration of the project.

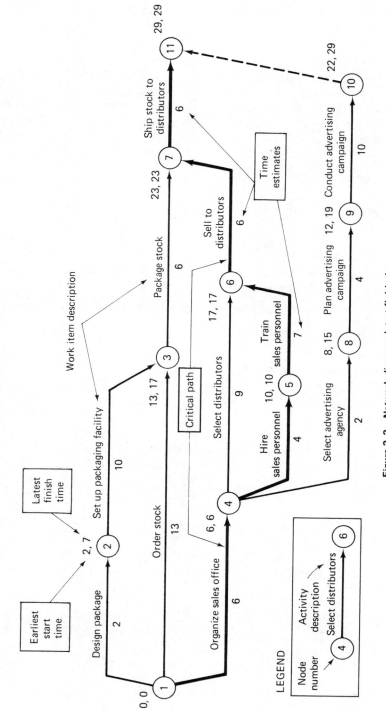

Figure 3-3. Network diagram: latest finish time

LEGEND

Node number → Activity description → Select distributors

TOTAL FLOAT

From the scheduling viewpoint, one of the major advantages of network analysis is that it identifies the jobs that have optional starting and finishing dates. These jobs have *total float*, which is the difference between the time available for performing a job and the time required for doing it.

Computation

Total float is equal to:

- Time *available* for performing the job — Time *required* for performing the job.
- Time *available* for performing the job = Latest finish time (LF) – Earliest start time (ES).
- Time *required* for performing the job = Time estimate.

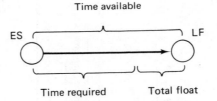

For example, using this formula, the total float for Job 4,6 on the product introduction project would be

$$(17 - 9) - 6 = 2 \text{ days of total float}$$

Another way to express total float can be seen in the illustration below. The time available for Job 4,6 is the difference between the latest finish time and the earliest start time. The time estimate for Job 4,6 is subtracted from the time available to determine the total float.

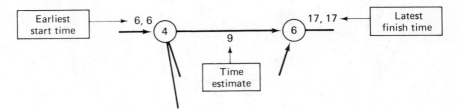

Total float figures are vital in scheduling a project. They indicate which jobs have no float and cannot be delayed without extending the length of the project. Equally important, they show which jobs have some leeway in scheduling. (See Figure 3-4.)

You will note that jobs which have no float are marked with an asterisk (*). These jobs are on the critical path, and their sum makes up the longest path on the network in terms of time requirements.

It must be pointed out, however, that the total float figures must be used with care. For example, there are 4 days of total float available for Job 1,3 of the product introduction project. If this total float is used by scheduling Job 1,3 to begin at time 4, the 4 days of float will not be available for Job 3,7 which is also shown to have 4 days of total float. Job 3,7 must then be scheduled to begin at time 17. It cannot be scheduled to begin at time 13, its earliest start time, because the total float has already been used on Job 1,3.

Total float figures thus indicate all the places where float is available and may indicate the same float at more than one place. There

Activity (node numbers)	Latest finish time	(−)	Earliest start time	(−)	Time estimate for completing job	=	Total float
1, 2	7	(−)	0	(−)	2	=	5
1, 3	17		0		13		4
1, 4	6		0		6		0*
2, 3	17		2		10		5
3, 7	23		13		6		4
4, 6	17		6		9		2
4, 5	10		6		4		0*
5, 6	17		10		7		0*
6, 7	23		17		6		0*
4, 8	15		6		2		7
8, 9	19		8		4		7
9, 10	29		12		10		7
7, 11	29		23		6		0*
10, 11**	29		22		0		7

* Critical path.

** Dummy—has no time duration.

Figure 3-4. Computation of total float

are two other types, free float and independent float, which tend to clarify this situation. These types of float will be defined later.

Where to Use Float

At what point should total float be taken when jobs are being scheduled? This decision is based on such factors as requirements for various resources, effect on cost, stability of employment, and cost penalties that may be incurred if certain jobs are delayed. For example, in the project introduction project, the float available on Job 9,10 (Conduct Advertising Campaign) would probably be used to delay its completion until the last possible moment. The advertising campaign should coincide more with the sales made by the distributors. Scheduling decisions of this kind within the framework of the float considerations can be made throughout the project.

FREE AND INDEPENDENT FLOAT

Float is defined as the time the performance of a job may be delayed without delaying overall project completion. If a job is on the critical path, it has no float. On all other paths in the diagram, some slippage is permissible without delaying project completion. Float figures make it possible to identify jobs that have optional starting and finishing dates. The determination of float for these jobs is important in order to identify the various scheduling operations which the scheduler may use to better allocate money, labor, and other resources to the project.

There are three types or definitions of float: total, free, and independent.

Total float is the least restrictive definition of float. The calculation of total float tells the scheduler all the jobs in the network on which float might be taken. It must be remembered that the same float will be shown on the chain of activities along the same path.

Free float figures have the advantage that each occurrence of float is recorded only once in a project. The effect of free-float computations is to "push" the float to the last job in the chain of activities in which the float occurs.

Independent float data isolate the float that is available on one job and one job only. It is calculated on the assumption that all previous jobs are scheduled as late as possible and all succeeding jobs as early as possible.

Each type of float has some drawbacks in application, but when all three are considered together, they provide valuable data for effectively scheduling a project. Before defining these in more detail, let us define the major factors in the float calculations:

1. *Earliest Start Time* (ES): earliest time any job can be scheduled, assuming that all previous jobs were completed on time.

   The project duration is equal to the earliest start time of the ending node of the last activity in the project.

2. *Latest Finish Time* (LF): latest time that a job can be completed without lengthening the duration of the project. The latest finish time is required in identifying the critical path and in calculating float for jobs in the network.

3. *Total Float* (TF): the difference between the maximum time available for performing a job and the estimated time required for doing it.

   - The same total float may be recorded for more than one activity in a path.

   - If all total float is taken, all following activities in that path become critical.

4. *Free Float* (FF): the delay possible in an activity if all preceding jobs start as early as possible while allowing all subsequent jobs to start at their earliest time.

THE FORMULA FOR FREE FLOAT (JOB X)

$$\text{Free float} = \begin{bmatrix} \text{Earliest start time} \\ \text{for jobs immediately} \\ \text{following Job } X \end{bmatrix}$$
$$- \begin{bmatrix} \text{Earliest start} \\ \text{time for Job } X \end{bmatrix} - \begin{bmatrix} \text{Duration} \\ \text{of Job } X \end{bmatrix}$$

Free float is recorded selectively in the project. The effect of free float calculations is to "push" the float to the last activity in the chain in which the float occurs.

   - Free float is recorded for one activity only; thus, free float provides a safety factor.

   - Available float is shown only on the last activity.

5. *Independent Float* (IF): the delay possible in an activity if all preceding jobs are completed as late as possible and all sub-

sequent jobs are to be started at the earliest possible start time.

The purpose of calculating independent float is to isolate where float must be used on one job and is not available to any other job.

INDEPENDENT FLOAT FOR JOB X

$$\text{Independent float} = \begin{bmatrix} \text{Earliest start time} \\ \text{for jobs immediately} \\ \text{succeeding Job } X \end{bmatrix}$$

$$- \begin{bmatrix} \text{Latest finish time} \\ \text{for jobs immediately} \\ \text{preceding Job } X \end{bmatrix} - \begin{bmatrix} \text{Duration} \\ \text{of Job } X \end{bmatrix}$$

- If the result is negative, independent float for Job X = 0.
- Independent float isolates the float that is available on one job and one job only. The calculations are based on all previous jobs and are scheduled as late as possible, and all succeeding jobs are scheduled as early as possible.

Examples of free float and independent float using the product introduction project are shown in Figure 3–5.

Calculations for Latest Start and Earliest Finish

Determining optional starting and finishing times for project activities can be of some benefit to the scheduler. Both optional starting and finishing times are related to the total float value of each project activity.

Latest start = Earliest start + Total float

Earliest finish = Latest finish – Total float

The schedule tabulation for the product introduction project shown in Figure 3–6 illustrates all the optional dates: the earliest and latest starts as well as the earliest and latest finishes of the project jobs.

FREE FLOAT

i, j	Description of job X	Earliest start time of succeeding activities	(−)	Earliest start time of job X	(−)	Duration of job X	=	Free float		
4, 8	Select advertising agency	(Job 8, 9) plan advertising campaign		(Job 4, 8) select advertising agency		(Job 4, 8)	=			
		8		6		2	=	0		
8, 9	Plan advertising campaign	(Job 9, 10) conduct advertising campaign		(Job 8, 9) plan advertising campaign		(Job 8, 9)				
		12		8		4	=	0		
9, 10	Conduct advertising campaign	(Job 10, 11) dummy		(Job 9, 10) conduct advertising campaign		(Job 9, 10)				
		22		12		10	=	0	=	7*
10, 11	Dummy	(End of job)		(Job 10, 11) dummy		(Job 10, 11)				
		29		22		0	=	7		

*Where a dummy is at the end of the chain of activities, the free-float value is transferred to the preceding job activity.

INDEPENDENT FLOAT

i, j	Description of job X	Earliest start time of succeeding activities	(−)	Latest finish time of preceding activity	(−)	Duration of job X	=	Independent float		
1, 4	Organize sales office	(Job 4, 6) select distributors (Job 4, 5) hire sales personnel (Job 4, 8) select advertising agency		Start of job		(Job 1, 4)				
		6		0		6	=	0		
2, 3	Set up packaging facility	(Job 3, 7) package stock		(Job 1, 2) design package		(Job 2, 3)				
		13		7		10	=	−4	=	0*
4, 6	Select distributors	(Job 6, 7) sell to distributors		(Job 1, 4) organize sales office		(Job 4, 6)				
		17		6		9	=	2		
5, 6	Train sales personnel	(Job 6, 7) sell to distributors		(Job 4, 5) hire sales personnel		(Job 5, 6)				
		17		10		7	=	0		

*A negative independent float is equal to zero independent float.

Figure 3–5. Calculating free float and independent float

SUMMARY

An important part of the project scheduling phase is time estimating, which involves getting a time estimate for each job in the project. The time estimate represents the amount of time an experienced person thinks the job will require under specified conditions. The first set of time estimates is generally made on the assumption that the project will be accomplished on a normal basis (employing readily available resources and using a minimum of overtime and other special measures). If the project duration based on the first set of time estimates does not meet project objectives, a second set of estimates is obtained. Reduc-

i, j	Description	Time (weeks)	Earliest Start	Earliest Finish	Latest Start	Latest Finish	Float Total	Float Free	Float Independent
1, 2	Design package	2	0	2	5	7	5	0	0
1, 3	Order stock	13	0	13	4	17	4	0	0
1, 4	Organize sales office	6	0	6	0	6	0	0	0
2, 3	Set up packaging facility	10	2	12	7	17	5	1	0
3, 7	Package stock	6	13	19	17	23	4	4	0
4, 5	Hire sales personnel	4	6	10	6	10	0	0	0
4, 6	Select distributors	9	6	15	8	17	2	2	2
4, 8	Select advertising agency	2	6	8	13	15	7	0	0
5, 6	Train sales personnel	7	10	17	10	17	0	0	0
6, 7	Sell to distributors	6	17	23	17	23	0	0	0
7, 11	Ship stock to distributors	6	23	29	23	29	0	0	0
8, 9	Plan advertising campaign	4	8	12	15	19	7	0	0
9, 10	Conduct advertising campaign	10	12	22	19	29	7	7	7
10, 11	Dummy	0	22	22	29	29	7	7	0

Figure 3–6. Schedule tabulation

tions are made in time estimates by expediting jobs on the critical path; in this way, the project duration is brought within the project deadline.

During the project, revised time estimates may be necessary if the progress of work varies from the schedule. When delays occur, time must be removed from some remaining jobs to assure that the project will be completed on schedule. If work is progressing ahead of schedule, adjustments may be made to shorten the overall duration of the project.

The timing calculations provide information necessary to effectively schedule a project. For small projects, calculations can be made manually; for larger projects, a computer is used. In the first series of calculations, the earliest start time at each node in the network is determined. The earliest start time at a node is the earliest time any job can be scheduled to start from that node.

The computation of the earliest start times also yields the project duration. This duration is checked against project objectives. If it does not meet project objectives, the duration must be compressed by expediting some of the critical jobs on the project.

The latest finish time for each node on the network is then calculated. This is the latest time that jobs can be completed without lengthening the duration of the project. The earliest start and latest finish times permit another calculation that yields the total float for each job — the difference between the time available for performing a job and the time required for performing it. The total float calculations make it possible to readily identify the critical path.

The benefits to be derived from the critical path timing calculations are principally: (1) the establishment of the project duration for the plan, (2) the identification of the longest path (critical path) through the project, and (3) the identification of jobs for which there is scheduling flexibility without lengthening project duration.

Float figures make it possible to identify jobs that have optional starting and finishing dates. Total float is the least restrictive definition of float. The calculation of total float tells the scheduler all the jobs in the network on which float might be taken. It must be remembered that the same float may be indicated on more than one job.

Free-float figures have the advantage that each occurrence of float is recorded only once in a project. The effect of free-float computations is to "push" the float to the last job in the chain of activities in which the float occurs.

Independent-float data isolate the float that is available on one job and one job only. It is calculated on the assumption that all previous jobs are scheduled as late as possible and all succeeding jobs as early as possible.

Each type of float — total, free, and independent — has some drawbacks in application, but when all three are considered together, they provide valuable data for effectively scheduling a project.

With the planning diagram, the list of critical activities, and the remainder of the jobs with their available float, the project can now be scheduled. The technique for developing a job schedule and monitoring the project is discussed in Chapter 4.

4

Project Control

Project control, the third phase of the project management cycle, generally consists of continuously monitoring the progress of each project item, then taking the necessary action on those items shown to be "drifting" to keep the project on the planned schedule. One of the best expedients used by those keeping track of job progress is the bar chart. Actions taken on a daily basis are shown on the detailed bar chart schedule. For management review on a weekly or monthly basis, a summary bar chart is prepared which is based on the detailed time schedule. In this chapter we construct a bar chart schedule, develop a summary bar chart as a communication aid in a project status report, and prepare a complete project status report.

CONSTRUCTING A BAR CHART SCHEDULE

The network diagram is excellent for laying out and planning a job. It is very useful in visualizing the status of the job by highlighting the critical items and potential bottlenecks. Its importance lies in showing the interrelationships among the project. However, for scheduling jobs, the network analysis technique does have some limitations:

1. Often, the network is difficult to interpret.

2. A great deal of time is usually needed to prepare changes. These changes will also require a great deal of time for making modifications to the network diagram.

3. A network makes it difficult to note estimated costs versus actual costs.

4. Individual skills are not recognized.

A bar chart recognizes the scheduling limitations when using network analysis; however, its construction needs the information derived from the network analysis calculations. To illustrate this, the bar chart time schedule for the sample problem, "A New Product

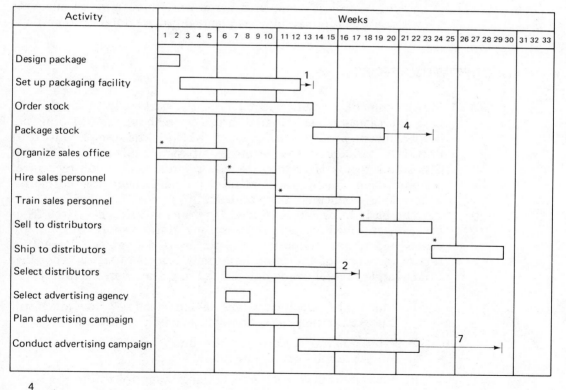

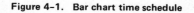

*Critical path activities.

Figure 4-1. Bar chart time schedule

Introduction," is shown in Figure 4–1. The procedure for construct-ing this bar chart is as follows:

1. Use the earliest start time of each project activity.

2. The length of each bar is the duration of each activity.

3. Plot one activity per line. In some cases it may be advan-tageous to plot a number of activities on one line. If the critical path items are shown on one line, a change to the planned schedule of each of the items and the effect on the project duration can be immediately noted.

4. Designate the free-float time on the bar chart. This provides a visual examination of any schedule flexibility in case the actual timing of a project item tends to deviate from the timing plan. (Examining the activity path, where the free float occurs, will show the amount of "drifting" that is permissible for a project item; in other words, there may be adequate float time to maintain the planned project duration time.)

PROJECT STATUS REPORT

Project control is predicated on an early start–early finish philoso-phy, the same as that initiated in project scheduling. This principle is used in the *project status report*, which is the discipline used to provide a periodic factual record as a basis for management action. The status report is used to maneuver, guide, anticipate, recognize, evaluate, and finally recommend to management the corrective action on any indicated delay or drift.

The basic information needed for project control is derived from the project schedule, and the resulting status report will employ charts and graphs to portray the status of the project. Exception reporting is one of the most important aspects of status reporting. For example, the following points need to be raised in the report:

1. Which jobs, specifically, are behind schedule? How much will this extend the project completion date if not corrected?

2. What are the reasons for the delays that have caused the project to fall behind schedule?

3. What steps have been or are being taken to restore the situa-tion, and what results have been obtained or are expected?

4. What are your recommendations for further action that will restore the corrected situation?

Summary Bar Chart

A *summary bar chart* is an excellent communication device to apprise management of the status of the project. How it is summarized from the bar chart schedule, and the manner in which the current status is described, will determine how well it is accepted by management. For example, an excellent outline to illustrate progress of an engineering project is through its project cycle, which usually evolves through these phases:

1. Feasibility study
2. Management approval
3. Basic engineering
4. Design and procurement
5. Construction
6. Equipment installation
7. Startup

There is also an analogy between the phases of an engineering project and projects in other fields. The size and complexity of the project will determine whether all of these phases needed to be included in the summary.

An illustration of the summary bar chart is shown in Figure 4-2 using the sample problem, "A New Product Introduction."

The bar chart introduces some features that may require explanations, either in the form of a legend noted on the chart or in a supplemental attachment. For example, the summary chart in Figure 4-2 requires the following explanation:

1. The rectangular bars (⬜) represent the project phases (design, purchase order, fabrication, installation, tryout, etc.) of each major item in a timing sequence to meet the projected completion date. The portion that is completed is filled in (▬).

2. Critical project event dates or milestones (▽) are left hollow until that event is completed, and then are filled in (▼).

3. The planned program completion milestone (▽) is shown in the upper right of the chart. If the completion milestone requires a time change because of changes in scope, technical problems, late deliveries, and so on, the updated completion milestone will be noted with a dashed line (▽).

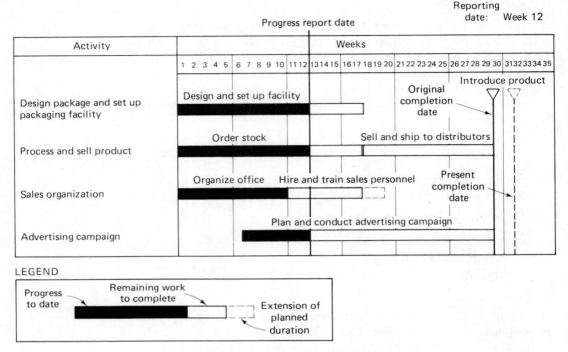

Figure 4-2. **Summary bar chart**

A review of the work activities at the end of the 12th week indicated the following status:

	Based on Earliest Start Time	Total Float
Design Package and Set Up Packaging Facility	Behind 2 weeks	5 weeks
Order Stock	Behind 3 weeks	4 weeks
Hire and Train Sales Personnel	Behind 2 weeks	0 weeks
Plan and Conduct Advertising Campaign	Behind 4 weeks	7 weeks

Based on earliest start times and the available total float, the present status of the work activity group, Hire and Train Sales Personnel, affects the completion date at the present rate of progress. This project will be completed 2 weeks later than planned.

Contents of a Status Report

The status report is a reflection of the program content in a summary outline form. It contains the status of key project items, an assessment of these items, and those items that should be given special attention. Specifically, a "full-blown" project status report will contain the following documents:

- Cover letter
- Executive highlights
- Summary of project
  a. Bar chart
  b. Project status
  c. Milestone report

(Examples of these documents are shown at the end of this chapter. See Figures 4-4, 4-5, and 4-6.)

The *cover letter* is addressed to the management personnel whose activity is participating or has other interest in the particular project. Its contents briefly explain the program of the job, anticipated completion dates of major events, brief statements concerning the status of critical items, and potential solutions to any problems.

Executive highlights will underline the status of the important aspects of the project. Highlights can be in the form of a "bullet" listing (●); it should also consist of a brief sentence or two, without going into too much detail. In brief progress status reports, executive highlights may sometimes be incorporated in the cover letter.

The *project summary* includes a bar chart that combines the work activities in a graphic form in such a manner that management can review the overall project and be spared the countless details associated with day-by-day activity. It applies the management by exception principle, which allows more attention to the critical items.

The steps in reporting to management through the summary chart are:

1. Show the actual program status compared to the plan.
2. Revise time estimates, if required. Portray graphically any extensions beyond the planned completion time.
3. Highlight critical items in the commentary below the bar chart. (See Figure 4-6.)
4. Introduce options to achieve objectives. If there is evidence

that the project completion will be delayed, show this possibility early in the project. If a delay in the project duration is inevitable, show the extent of delay on the bar chart.

The status commentary below the summary bar chart explains in more detail the status of the project items shown in the bar chart. As the summary bar chart graphically portrays the status of the major activities, the status commentary is used to highlight the details of these activities, with particular attention to those that are critical.

The milestone report on the summary sheet includes the planned dates of project start and completion, deviations from these dates, and explanation of the variances. Important interim dates of the project are also shown, as these dates are just as important as the major milestone dates to be met for the timely completion of the project.

The project status report may be one page or several pages. Its format may take on a different design than the one shown; however, the contents would be similar, and there may be additional special features, depending upon the project requirements. In any event, its contents will contain the essential data that management needs to appraise the project properly.

Milestones

Milestones are selected events that are of major importance toward achieving objectives. They are key events, usually showing the completion date of a major phase of the project, the delivery date of a major equipment item, or the date of a key management decision to make the project maintain its successful completion. These events may or may not be on the critical path.

The milestone approach is an excellent "tool" for reporting project status in summary form to higher management, as it summarizes the status of the major events.

In Figure 4-3 the milestones for the product introduction project are displayed. These milestones highlight the important events leading to the project completion date.

The milestones on a network diagram represent the key starting or completion dates of major events. The display of milestones on the network diagram can be helpful for summarizing the planning strategy; however, in most instances the milestone data can only be analyzed through the development of computer calculations.

The computer-oriented milestone technique provides a condensed version or summary to help direct the project to a successful

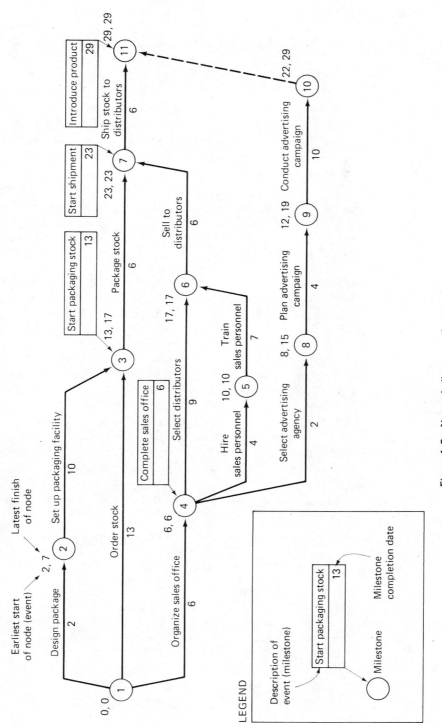

Figure 4-3. Network diagram: milestone chart

57

completion. It offers a number of advantages, such as:

- The milestone listing provides a precise form for program progress to be monitored. A computer printout provides a milestone listing for this purpose.

- The computer program can sort a milestone listing of behind-schedule activities, highlighting the items that must be expedited to ensure that the project can be completed on schedule.

- Additional milestones can be added during the course of the project. These are added to monitor a desired activity, to monitor a program leading to that activity, or to monitor the entire chain of preceding activities along that path to the point of the milestone event.

The technique used for monitoring the status of milestones is to "dam up" the time at the milestone, thereby not permitting any behind-schedule activities to pass that point in time. In the case of behind-schedule situations, each group of behind-schedule activities can be isolated, examined, and then brought back to schedule. (How one or several of these activities can be expedited to return the project to schedule will be discussed in a later chapter.) It is possible that as one group of activities is cleared up, another series requiring attention may present itself. Where the behind-schedule activities are quite prevalent, it is a constant whittling process. This technique is most effective when introduced in the early stages of the project. Corrective actions need to be taken at each milestone; otherwise, subsequent activities will be adversely affected and, in all probability, the objective will be missed.

The milestone approach is an effective tool; however, it is difficult to apply without the assistance of a computer.

SUMMARY

Project control, the third phase of the project management cycle, consists of monitoring the progress of the project activities, comparing them with the plan, and taking the required action where variances are shown.

The project status report is designed to inform management of project performance. The report should be designed so that management, in examining the status reports that are in condensed form, should be able to make sound project performance appraisal of the project. The report should also highlight the critical areas, and through applying the principle of management by exception, management can objectively evaluate the problem areas.

Project status reporting revolving around milestones is an effective application of the management by exception principle. The milestone approach isolates the behind-schedule activities so that corrective action can be taken early in the project. The use of the computer is necessary for deriving any analysis through the milestone approach.

Messrs.   August 17, 19___

SUBJECT: Status of Glass Program

A program based on tinting Tulsa No. 1 starting in early December, 19___ , has been finalized. It will provide for a timely supply of promotional samples for Sales and Marketing for the glass introduction program and for production shipments to start February 1. Tulsa's planned cycle pattern for the tint glass run is shown in the attached detail.

Equipment facilities and procurement are continuing on schedule but the two July trials at Tulsa were not completed and were inconclusive. Mechanical equipment malfunctions with the temporary exhaust system have since been corrected and the test unit is now ready for further on-line trials.

Program status highlights are attached.

Please advise if there are any questions.

                                                                      M. Spinner

MS/1rd
Attachments

Figure 4-4. Example—cover letter

- Fabrication of process equipment is over 75% completed, and about 60% of the assembly completed. "Debugging" at Tech Center, prior to shipment to Tulsa, is expected to begin October 1.

- Equipment tryout will start November 15; by December 1, Manufacturing expects to confirm ability to produce acceptable product.

- Based on Tulsa No. 1 operating on tint in December, glass shipments are projected to start by February 1.

- Research and Development, Glass Tech Center, will provide Sales and Marketing with initial promotional samples for mailing campaign. The 3" x 4" seamed edge glass samples will be completed by December 1.

- Timetable for supplying other glass samples for the Marketing introduction program is based on tinting Tulsa No. 1 furnace in early December.

Glass Engineering
8-4

Figure 4-5. Example—executive highlights

Figure 4-6.
Project sum-
mary: bar chart,
project status,
and milestone
report

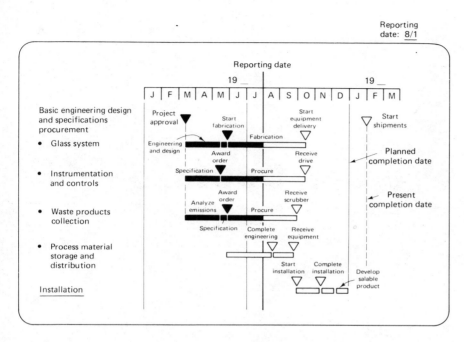

Progress to Date

There has been little development progress at Tulsa in the past two months. Most of the on-line trial
on-line trial malfunctions have been caused by mechanical difficulties, which are being
corrected for the scheduled August trials. Procurement of facility equipment is on schedule,
with no critical delivery problems existing at this time. Progress details of major items are as
follows:

Glass process equipment — Fabrication, about 75% complete, is planned to be ready for
"debugging" by October 15 at the Tech Center prior to shipment to Tulsa. Required for
"debugging": the air control panel is now being fabricated and the electrical control panel
order was awarded July 25. Both panels are expected to be completed and shipped to the
Tech Center in September.

Exhaust and waste collection — Duct work should be completed by August 1, to the Glass
Tech Center for assembly. Supplier of the special air scrubber confirms Tulsa delivery by
October 15.

Process material storage, mixing, and distribution — Behind schedule condition due to
lengthy negotiations. Supplier's quotation is considered extensive. To avoid production
delay, Tulsa will assume responsibility and provide temporary systems.

Milestone Report

Schedules remain the same as last report, installation of equipment expected to be completed
November 15, as planned. Production start date of February 1 is contingent on present plan
for tinting at Tulsa in December.

November 15	Complete equipment installation; start tryout (on clear glass line).
December 5	Begin tinting Tulsa #1.
January 15	Provide marketing with glass for trade shows, model homes, etc.
February 1	Start production shipments.

5

Project Costs

To many in management, the costs associated with a project may be more important than the timing aspects, and they have a great impact on how the project is carried out. Project costs are usually concerned with the flow of cash or movement of money throughout the various groups connected with the project. The owner or company officer financing the project is interested and must be made knowledgeable of these two main considerations:

1. What total amounts of money will be needed over the course of the project?

2. When will the money be needed to make payments for materials, labor, and other expenses over the duration of the project?

An accurate determination of the funds allocated to the project and controlling these funds throughout the project are important to the financial integrity of the organization.

This chapter is devoted to three aspects of project costs:

- Project cost schedule
- Project cost control (indicated cost outcome)
- Cost minimizing (time/cost trade-offs)

Although these three aspects do not represent the total cost implications of a project, they do cover the more important cost areas. Persons directly associated with project operations should be aware that successful management of costs is essential to proper project management.

The initial effort involves the development of costs for each project item. Project costs are established for each work activity in the same manner as the timing for the project was developed. As is the case in developing timing estimates, it is best for those knowledgeable of the specific work items to furnish the cost estimates. The derivation of these estimates may range from firm supplier or contractor quotations to establishing costs from concepts alone. In any event, the project costs that are established during the planning phase are those generally used for budget purposes. Therefore, it is important to use the best possible estimates, as these costs become "sacred." The total of the project work activities represents the variable costs of the project budget.

In many instances there is also a fixed total cost. If, during the planning phase, the project costs are more than what was allowed in the budget, the costs are reviewed again and revised until they meet the budget objectives.

PROJECT COST SCHEDULE

The principal reasons for scheduling costs are the following:

1. To assist the financial group in funding the project. By projecting its cash flow through a cost schedule, finance personnel will know when and how much of the funds will be needed at any period of time.

2. To assist the project management team in developing the expenditure distribution over the life of the project. Once the project is underway, this planned distribution can be compared with actual costs.

3. The financial activity will also use the cost schedule for property tax purposes and depreciation schedules.

4. Project cost schedules become the basis for determining timing for various property tax payments.

The procedure for developing a cost schedule is as follows:

Step 1. Complete the bar chart time schedule.

Step 2. Prepare a tabulation format to determine the cost slope (the cost/time unit).

Step 3. Determine the time increments at which costs are to be considered. (This is usually 1 month. Shorter periods of time imply that costs are critical; longer periods suggest that costs are not critical.)

Step 4. Prepare a tabulation format to determine costs (or expenditures) for the time increments.

Step 5. Total the expenditures for each time increment.

Step 6. Total the expenditures for all the time increments, which represents the total project cost.

Step 7. Plot the total for each time increment on a cost distribution graph using the bar chart time schedule.

Adjustments to the timing schedule may be necessary after an analysis of the cost schedule is made. The procedure described above has a number of advantages which will allow a good cost analysis to be made.

Once the bar chart time schedule is completed, the next step in developing a cost schedule is to prepare the cost slope for each project job. The *cost slope* is equal to the cost incurred in performing a job activity per unit length of time. A suggested format to prepare the cost slope is shown as follows:

COST SLOPE

Activity	Total Cost (Dollars)	Duration (Weeks)	Cost Slope (Dollars/Week)
(1)	(2)	(3)	(4)

Specific Instructions

Column	*Instructions*
(1) Activity	Enter the description of the project activity.
(2) Total Cost	Enter the total cost in dollars of performing the project activity.
(3) Duration	Enter the total duration time of the project activity. The unit used will be determined by the requirements of the project. Usually, 1-month increments are adequate; however, a smaller unit of

time is used if the project costs become critical.

(4) Cost Slope   Enter the result of dividing column (2) by column (3).

Once the cost slope is calculated, the next step is to determine the total amount of expenditures that the project incurs per unit of time (week or month is a common timing base). The necessary prerequisites for this step (as in the case of calculating the cost slope) is to have completed the network analysis, since the network diagram is used as a basis to prepare the bar chart time schedule. This schedule is the important base document that is required to be used in conjunction with the total monthly (or weekly) project expenditures. A suggested format for project expenditures is as follows:

COST SCHEDULE

Time Period	Activity	Activity Time (Weeks)	Cost Slope (Dollars/Week)	Expenditures (Dollars)
(5)	(6)	(7)	(8)	(9)

Specific Instructions

Column	*Instructions*
(5) Time Period	Enter the period of time that is desired to determine the expenditures. (Usually, 1-month periods are used; however, if project costs appear critical, 2-week periods may be required. In any event, the time period should remain constant.)
(6) Activity	Enter the description of the project activity.
(7) Activity Time	Enter the time units that the activity performs within the time period.
(8) Cost Slope	Enter the cost slope that was developed previously.
(9) Expenditures	Enter the result of multiplying column (7) by column (8). Total the expenditures within each time period, and enter the total for each period before starting the next time period.

The total cost of the project will equal the sum of the total time period expenditures. The expenditures developed from this cost schedule format will serve as the basis for calculating the variance from actual project expenditures during a given time period.

As an additional expedient the bar chart schedule and the cost distribution graph can be used to develop a graphic portrayal of the project costs for each time period.

Adjustments to the timing schedule may be necessary after making an analysis of the cost schedule and the cost distribution graph. Changes of this type during the planning period are most beneficial, as many problems associated with time/cost relationships can be resolved before the project gets under way. Spending modifications after the project starts may also require scheduling changes, and the bar chart cost schedule with the cost distribution graph will be helpful in the replanning of the project.

When scheduling changes due to project costs are required, the first approach is to examine the activities having float times so that the project duration time is not affected.

The sample problem, "A New Product Introduction," will be used to illustrate the procedure in setting up a cost schedule.

1. *Finding the Cost Slope:* The cost estimate for each project item had been determined previously and the total project budget is the sum of the project item costs. The first step is the development of the cost slope, which in this problem will be the weekly costs for each project item. (Development of the cost slope is shown in Figure 5-1.)

2. *Developing the Cost Schedule:* Totaling the expenditures for each 5 weeks of the project was selected as the most appropriate for this project. The initial cost schedule for the product introduction project shows the following cash flow for each 5-week period:

Weeks	Total Cost
0–5	$31,770
6–10	46,050
11–15	52,484
16–20	61,998
21–25	42,198
26–29	6,000

Development of the above expenditures for each 5-week period is shown in Figure 5-2. The basis of the above cost schedule in the bar chart is shown in Figure 5-1.

3. *Constructing the Cost Distribution Graph (from the Bar*

Project activity	Cost (dollars)	Duration (weeks)	Cost slope (dollars/week)
Design package	$ 7,500	2	$ 3,750
Order stock	2,000	13	154
Organize sales office	12,000	6	2,000
Set up packaging facility	45,000	10	4,500
Package stock	6,000	6	1,000
Hire sales personnel	8,000	4	2,000
Select distributors	13,000	9	1,444
Select advertising agency	4,000	2	2,000
Train sales personnel	28,000	7	4,000
Sell to distributors	64,000	6	10,666
Ship stock to distributors	9,000	6	1,500
Plan advertising campaign	6,000	4	1,500
Conduct advertising campaign	36,000	10	3,600
Total	$240,500		

Figure 5-1. Calculating the cost slope (cost/week)

Chart Time Schedule): The bar chart time schedule and the 5-week cost distribution graph are shown in Figure 5–3.

The time schedule for the activities is based on the earliest start times. For making adjustments to the schedule, the free float is shown on the bar chart, thus allowing changes to be made on the chart within the planned project duration.

4. *Making Schedule Adjustments to Allow More Uniform Cost Distribution* (see Figure 5–4): It appears that disbursements in the 16-20-week period are appreciably higher than the other cost periods, and reducing the cash flow in this period may be important to the financial arrangements made for this project. For example, credit procurement may be premised on more even monthly disbursements.

Examining this project reveals that the advertising sequence (or chain), which has high unit costs, has a 7-week float. Pushing "Conducting the Advertising Campaign" to its latest start not only helps in arriving at a more uniform cash flow, but permits the campaign to be under way as close to the end of the project as possible.

Period	Activity	Activity time (weeks)	Cost slope (dollars/week)	Total activity expenditures (dollars)
0–5	Design package	2	$ 3,750	$ 7,500
	Order stock	5	154	770
	Set up packaging facility	3	4,500	13,500
	Organize sales office	5	2,000	10,000
	Total 0–5			$31,770
6–10	Order stock	5	154	770
	Set up packaging facility	5	4,500	22,500
	Organize sales office	1	2,000	2,000
	Hire sales personnel	4	2,000	8,000
	Select distributors	4	1,444	5,776
	Select advertising agency	2	2,000	4,000
	Plan advertising campaign	2	1,500	3,000
	Total 6–10			$46,046
11–15	Order stock	3	154	462
	Set up packaging facility	2	4,500	9,000
	Package stock	2	1,000	2,000
	Train sales personnel	5	4,000	20,000
	Select distributors	5	1,444	7,220
	Plan advertising campaign	2	1,500	3,000
	Conduct advertising campaign	3	3,600	10,800
	Total 11–15			$52,482
16–20	Package stock	4	1,000	4,000
	Train sales personnel	2	4,000	8,000
	Sell to distributors	3	10,666	31,998
	Conduct advertising campaign	5	3,600	18,000
	Total 16–20			$61,998
21–25	Sell to distributors	3	10,666	31,998
	Ship to distributors	2	1,500	3,000
	Conduct advertising campaign	2	3,600	7,200
	Total 21–25			$42,198
26–29	Ship to distributors	4	1,500	6,000
	TOTAL PROJECT COSTS			$240,500

Figure 5–2. Calculating the cost schedule

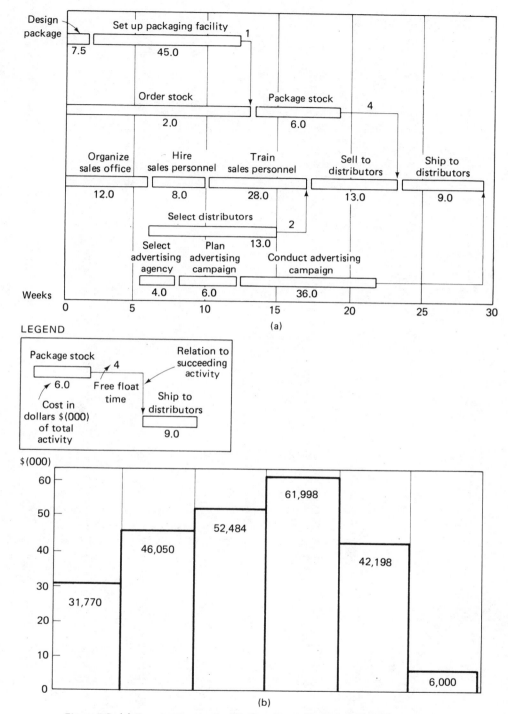

Figure 5-3. (a) Bar chart cost schedule [total cost for each work activity is noted below the corresponding bar] ; (b) Cost distribution graph

Conduct advertising campaign (use latest start)

Period (weeks)	Activity	Actual time (weeks)	Cost slope (dollars/week)	Expenditures (dollars)
16–20	Package stock	4	$ 1,000	$ 4,000
	Train sales personnel	2	4,000	8,000
	Sell to distributors	3	10,666	31,998
	Conduct advertising campaign	1	3,600	3,600
				$47,598
21–25	Sell to distributors	3	10,666	31,998
	Ship to distributors	2	1,500	3,000
	Conduct advertising campaign	5	3,600	18,000
				$53,998
26–29	Ship to distributors	4	1,500	6,000
	Conduct advertising campaign	4	3,600	14,400
				$20,400

Figure 5–4. Revised project costs

Weeks	Total Cost
0–5	$31,770
6–10	46,050
11–15	52,484
16–20	47,598
21–25	53,998
26–29	20,440

5. *Constructing the Revised Bar Chart Schedule and Revised Cost Distribution Graph:* The revised bar chart time schedule and the graphic display of the expenditures reflecting the adjusting of the advertising campaign schedule are shown in Figure 5–5.

PROJECT COST CONTROL

In the same manner as the project timing schedule, the status of project costs will be required periodically as the project is under way. As a management by exception application, a procedure should be established that can predict overspending (or cost overruns) as soon as they can be discovered.

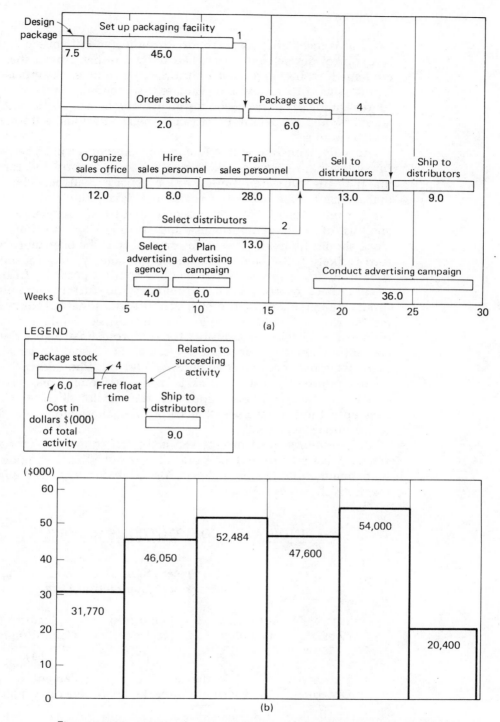

Figure 5-5. (a) Revised bar chart cost schedule; (b) Revised cost distribution graph

The project cost status report or indicated cost outcome report is a control device that is designed to ensure that project spending is contained within approved (authorized) amounts. Specifically, the report is used to review and evaluate this spending status of projects; to determine if project commitments are in line with authorized amounts; and to determine if (and when) additional authorizations may be required.

Usually, someone with a financial background will be responsible for preparing, reviewing, and evaluating these reports and for ensuring that the projected (indicated) costs are realistic. The project management team needs to provide the data when a potential overrun (or underrun) is first disclosed; at that time, a special review and analysis of open commitments and uncompleted portions of the work should be made. If it is determined that the overrun (or underrun) is likely to be beyond allowable tolerances, a request should be submitted for a project supplement as soon as possible. In the case of a project overrun beyond tolerance, no further commitments should be made against the project until additional authorized funding is obtained. It is possible that authorized funding cannot be obtained until those responsible for the project can assure the financial authorities that the total project costs can be contained. If no such assurance occurs, the project could be "shut down" while a complete project cost analysis is made. Although this may sound drastic, it may be a better approach than prolonging the cost overruns until the project goes "bankrupt" and there are no more funds to continue the project.

The submission of project status reports to management and the financial activity should be done on a regular basis. A good status reporting method is the *Indicated Cost Outcome Report*. A suggested format is shown as follows:

INDICATED COST OUTCOME REPORT

Date: _____

Project Start Date: _____

Project Completion Date: _____

Project Item	Authorized (Budgeted)	Committed to Date	Future Commitments
(1)	(2)	(3)	(4)

Indicated Outcome	Variance (Over) or (Under)	Percent (Over) or (Under)
(5)	(6)	(7)

Specific Instructions

Column	*Instructions*
(1) Project Item	Enter the description with each project job activity. (There may be several items included with some activities. In this case, they should also be itemized.)
(2) Authorized (Budgeted)	Enter the estimated dollar amount that has been developed and approved for completing the project activity item. There may be firm quotations that make up this item. If so, the estimate may be satisfactory to list without any added funds or contingency.

A word on contingency: A general rule that should be followed is: never estimate an item that cannot be reported. This applies to time estimates as well. Contingency is an item that cannot be reported. If there are uncertainties, the project item includes a predetermined added amount within the estimate. Your own internal detail must include this as a separate item. It could be noted as potential added work items, potential design changes, and so on.

The total costs for each of the project items may also be termed as a budget. The sum of the authorized costs equals the project budget. In most cases the project budget is not compatible with the manner in which an accounting procedure is usually structured. In a project detail each item may have certain account numbers assigned to it and they are used for various purposes. The project costs become the permanent capital investment base. They are also used for tax purposes and such expense items as depreciation. Other accounts may be associated with various operating expense accounts.

(3) Committed
to Date

Enter for each activity the amount that has been spent and/or ordered as of the date of the report. When a major cost commitment is made, such as the time an award order is given to a major equipment supplier, an indicated cost outcome should be prepared.

(4) Future
Commitments

Enter the additional costs that will be needed to complete the activity. These projections are usually estimated.

(5) Indicated
Outcome

Enter the sum of column (3), *Committed to Date*, and column (4), *Future Commitments*, for each activity. This figure is compared to the authorized (or budgeted) amount to determine the cost performance of each item. All of the indicated outcomes of the activities are algebraically added, and this total is compared with the total budgeted cost.

(6) Variance

Enter the difference between column (2), *Authorized* amount, and column (5), *Indicated Outcome*. When the difference is over the authorized amount (known as the overrun) beyond a predescribed tolerance (usually 10%) of the authorized amount, project operations may be obligated to stop until there is assurance that no further overruns can be expected.

(7) Percent of Variance Over or Under (optional)

Enter the result of dividing the difference between column (2), *Authorized* amount, and column (5), *Indicated Outcome*, divided by column (2), *Authorized* amount. (Multiply by 100 to arrive at percent amounts.)

If a project is near the end of completion, overruns close to the 10% limit may be tolerable, but if the program is in the early stages, a more in-depth review is necessary. In many firms it may be the perogative of the controller to refuse to authorize any further spending as a project reaches an overrun stage. It is good practice to review the program at periodic intervals with top management to assure them that the program costs will be contained (or the strategy to be employed where program costs may become a problem).

SAMPLE PROBLEM: A NEW PRODUCT INTRODUCTION

The sample problem will be used to illustrate the procedure in setting up an indicated cost outcome report. For this example we have assumed that the project is in its 15th week and a tabulation of the project item costs to date are shown in Figure 5-6.

With the indicated cost outcome tabulation, the cost report would include a highlight section as shown in Figure 5-7. In this particular example the program cost overrun may be more than what can be tolerated at this period. Unless program costs are shown to be contained, the comptroller may elect to refuse authorization of any additional expenditures. This, in effect, will shut down the project.

Although this may seem harsh, the results would be more disastrous if these costs conditions were not acted upon as early as possible. Shutting down the project is not necessarily an arbitrary decision by the comptroller. There may not be any more funds available for the project other than the authorized amount. The indicated outcome report allows the comptroller to make decisions before the program costs are completely out of control.

Another cost status report that has popular use is an accumulative cost report. The chart shown in Figure 5-8 shows the total project cost status to date as well as the projected costs. It provides a graphic picture of the existing costs

Reporting date: Week 15
Start date: 0
Completion date: Week 29

Project item	Authorized (budgeted)	Committed to date	Future commitments	Indicated outcome	Variance (over) or under	% Variance (over) or under
Design package	$ 7,500	$ 8,000	$ —	$ 8,000	$(500)	(6.7)
Order stock	2,000	2,000	—	2,000	—	—
Organize sales office	12,000	10,500	—	10,500	1,500	8.3
Set up packaging facility	45,000	50,000	—	50,000	(5,000)	(11.1)
Package stock	6,000	1,500	3,000	4,500	1,500	25.0
Hire sales personnel	8,000	4,000	3,500	7,500	500	6.3
Select distributors	13,000	12,000	—	12,000	1,000	7.7
Select advertising agency	4,000	2,000	—	2,000	2,000	50.0
Train sales personnel	28,000	25,000	7,000	32,000	(4,000)	(14.3)
Sell to distributors	64,000	1,000	63,000	64,000	—	—
Ship to distributors	9,000	—	9,000	9,000	—	—
Plan advertising campaign	6,000	5,500	—	5,500	500	8.3
Conduct advertising campaign	36,000	10,000	36,000	46,000	(10,000)	(27.7)
Total	$240,500	$131,500	$121,500	$253,000	$(12,500)	(5.2)

Figure 5-6. Indicated cost outcome report (week 15)

LEGEND

Authorized — estimated dollar amount.
Committed to date — amount spent or committed to be spent to date.
Future commitments — funds still needed to complete activity.
Indicated outcome — sum of funds committed to date and future commitments.
Variance (over) or under — difference between authorized funds and indicated outcome funds.
Percent (over) or under — [variance divided by authorized funds] times 100.

Figure 5-7. In-dicated cost out-come—highlights

Reporting date: Week 15

- Project expenditures are 5.2% over budget.

- Commitments to date: 55% of total authorized.

- Project is 50% complete.

- Outstanding items that indicate high overruns.
  - a. Train sales personnel (14.3%)
  - b. Advertising campaign (27.7%)

Recommendations to reduce overruns:

a. Train sales personnel — projected expenditures, $7,000; total indicated cost, $32,000; variance, $4,000 over authorized amount.

Recommendation: Modify training program to permit sales personnel to complete course earlier. Reducing time of training program could reduce project costs by $3,000.

b. Conduct advertising campaign — projected expenditures, $36,000; total indicated cost, $36,000; variance $20,000 over authorized amount.

Recommendation: Revise TV commercials, reduce advertisements in trade periodicals for an $8,000 savings.

Detailed report on reducing overrun will be included in the next report.

compared to the plan as well as the anticipated cost outcome. The budget (authorized) costs are accumulated from the cost schedule in Figure 5-3.

COST MINIMIZING

Cost minimizing as related to network analysis is concerned with determining how to reduce the time required for completing a project with the least amount of added expense. Reducing the duration of a project would include the review of such items as overtime, extra personnel, and additional equipment. The cost minimizing technique may also be termed time/cost trade-offs or "crash" programs.

If it is decided that the project duration time is to be reduced, it will be necessary to obtain the following cost data for each project item:

1. The expenditures required for accomplishing the work on a "normal" time basis.

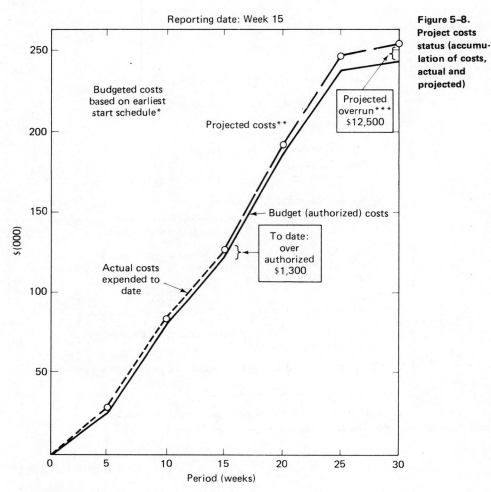

Reporting date: Week 15

Figure 5–8. Project costs status (accumulation of costs, actual and projected)

Budgeted costs based on earliest start schedule*

Projected costs**

Projected overrun*** $12,500

Budget (authorized) costs

To date: over authorized $1,300

Actual costs expended to date

$(000)

Period (weeks)

*See Figure 5-2.
**Projected costs—total funds needed to complete project.
***Projected overrun—additional funds required to complete project.

LEGEND

Period (weeks)	Budgeted costs	
	Cost	Accumulated cost
0 - 5	$31,770	$ —
6 - 10	46,050	77,820
11 - 15	52,484	130,304
16 - 20	61,998	192,302
21 - 25	42,198	234,500
26 - 29	6,000	240,500

2. The expenditures required for accomplishing the work on an expedited or "crash" basis. (It will also be necessary to obtain the reduction in time that served as a basis for these expenditures.)

The two sets of estimates will then be used to develop alternative schedules and, from these options, determine the best job schedule in terms of minimum additional cost.

The planning and scheduling functions are carried out for the project in the same manner as described in earlier chapters. The cost minimizing technique uses network analysis to develop the alternative schedules. Reviewing the steps in network analysis: first, state the objectives; second, determine the job activities and their interrelationships; third, prepare an arrow diagram; and finally, from the arrow diagram and the designated time estimates for each activity, calculate the timing for the initial schedule.

The following steps for cost minimizing purposes are taken:

1. Determine how much time each job can be reduced by "crashing" each job in the project.

2. Obtain the cost for accelerating the work.

From these data, the extra cost that will be incurred can be determined for reduced project duration times until the project is fully crashed. Also, from these data, the optimum project duration in terms of total cost can be determined, that is, the minimum amount of additional costs to achieve the best reduced project time.

Procedure

The cost minimizing procedure follows a "cut-and-try" pattern. For a large project, a computer is used to perform the calculations with great speed. However, the work can be done manually and the method shown is a manual arrangement. Once the arrow diagram has been developed, time estimates obtained, and the initial schedule calculated, the following steps are taken:

Step 1. *Direct Cost*

    a. Obtain the normal cost and the crash time and crash cost for each job in the network. Total the normal costs for each job to obtain the normal cost for the project.

    b. Determine the minimum cost for reducing the project duration by one time interval (such as a day or week).

This involves cutting back the duration of those jobs on the critical path that can be reduced at least expense. If more than one path is critical, this procedure is applied to all such paths.

c. Perform the same process to reduce the project duration a second time interval.

d. Repeat the process to a point where the project is "fully crashed" in terms of critical jobs.

Step 2. *Indirect Cost*

a. Determine the indirect cost for the project for the normal and crash times and for the time intervals between them.

Step 3. *Total Cost*

a. Add the direct to the indirect costs to determine the total cost at the various time intervals considered.

b. Identify the time interval, or project duration, at which the total cost will be at a minimum.

Network analysis is based on the premise that time and cost are interrelated. Most projects can be performed in a number of different ways from minimum cost–maximum time to minimum time–maximum cost. The method permits an educated choice between the two extremes, a choice that will be best for the particular operation under consideration.

Method for Calculating Cost Slope

The cost slope gives the rate of increase in cost for the decrease in time. To calculate the cost slope for each activity, four values are required for each activity:

1. *Normal Time:* job time estimate which assumes employment of the usual amount of labor, equipment, and so on.

2. *Normal Cost:* estimated expense for performing the project within the normal time estimate.

3. *Crash Time:* minimum estimated time in which a job could be completed if the job is accelerated by using one or more factors, such as overtime, extra labor, or additional equipment.

4. *Crash Cost:* normal cost plus the extra cost involved in applying those factors — overtime, extra labor, additional equipment.

These four factors are used to calculate the cost slope for each job, the increase in cost per unit of reduced project time:

$$\text{Cost slope} = \frac{\text{Crash cost} - \text{Normal cost}}{\text{Normal time} - \text{Crash time}}$$

Certain assumptions must be made in using the cost minimizing program to accelerate a project:

1. Crash time is always less than or equal to normal time.
2. Crash cost is always greater than or equal to normal cost.
3. The time/cost curve is generally linear, as illustrated in Figure 5-9.

If a more accurate approximation of the time/cost curve is desired, the job may be broken into two or more segments with a linear time/cost approximation for each segment. This is illustrated in Figure 5-10.

Establish the Final Schedule

Determining what the final schedule should be, in terms of reducing the project duration with a minimum overall project cost, can become quite complicated. For example, if the critical path is not much longer in time than other paths, a reduction in time for the critical path may cause one or more other paths to become critical. In many cases there may be a computer program available to provide the calculations more economically. The final schedule can then be established with the assurance that, based on the time estimates and

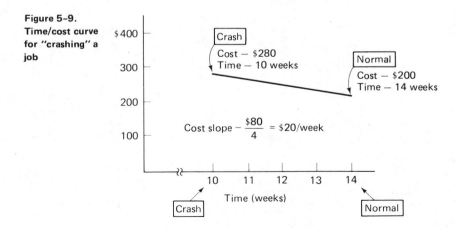

Figure 5-9.
Time/cost curve for "crashing" a job

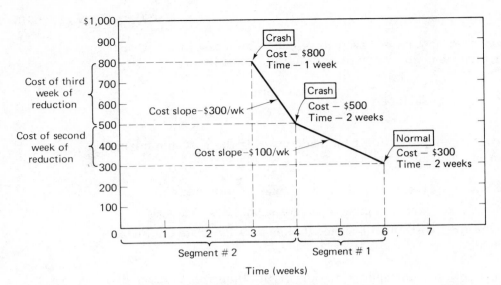

Figure 5-10. Segmented time/cost curve for a job

cost data, a minimum project cost will be incurred in meeting the specified deadline.

As a part of the process of establishing the final schedule, the computer is programmed to provide a minimum-cost curve for the project and the schedules corresponding to each point on this curve. Figure 5-11 shows the type of curve that can be printed out for a sample project.

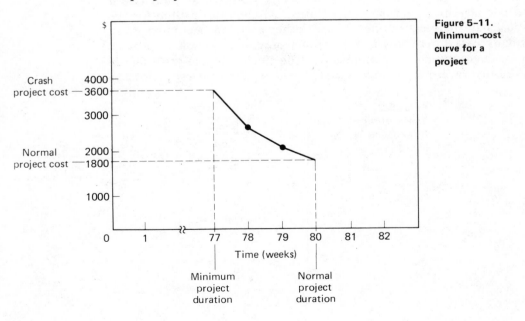

Figure 5-11. Minimum-cost curve for a project

82

EXAMPLE — OFFICE BUILDING[1]

The following example illustrates the procedure to be followed in applying cost minimizing to a project that is to be accelerated.

In this example an industrial plant office facility is to be rebuilt and expanded. The existing office abuts a manufacturing building in a highly congested industrial area. Since no new land is available, the existing office building must be demolished before the new building can be constructed in the cleaned area. For simplicity, the office building project has been subdivided into just 12 activities. The network diagram in Figure 5-12 reflects the logical flow of work in the project. Also shown is the tabulation of the normal time schedule of the project stating when each job must be done, when deliveries must take place, which are the critical jobs, and when the project will be completed (in this case, 65 days).

If the 65-day time duration is unacceptable, time can be saved by expediting one or more of the jobs along the critical path. This is more efficient than placing all jobs along the critical path on a crash basis. For each activity that is assigned a normal time duration, there is also a crash time duration — a minimum time in which the activity can be performed. For each of the time durations, there are also associated normal and crash costs. Once the normal crash times and costs are known, the cost slope for each activity can be determined.

$$\text{Cost slope} = \frac{\text{Crash cost} - \text{Normal cost}}{\text{Normal time} - \text{Crash time}}$$

The cost slope gives the rate of increase in cost for decrease in time. The cost data and the cost slope calculations are shown in Figure 5-13.

An intelligent choice of which job to expedite can be made by starting with compressing the time schedule of the critical job with the least-cost slope and then compressing the jobs with the lesser cost slope. In this example, the least-cost slope exists with Job 8,9, where a 2-day reduction can be effected at an additional cost of $1,000 per day. At this point Job 7,9 also becomes critical and any further reduction in Job 8,9 would also require a reduction in Job 7,9, which would increase the cost by $2,000 per day. Since Job 1,2 can be reduced in duration by 2 days at a cost of $1,400 per day, this job would be the next one to compress. Shown in Figure 5-14, this process is repeated until the project duration has been reduced to its minimum time of 47 days.

Since a decrease in project time requires additional capital expenditures, the direct costs obviously rise as the project time is decreased from 65 days. However, the total cost of this particular project is comprised of both direct costs and indirect costs.

[1] Adapted from *Architectural Record*, January 1963, © 1963, by McGraw-Hill, Inc., with all rights reserved.

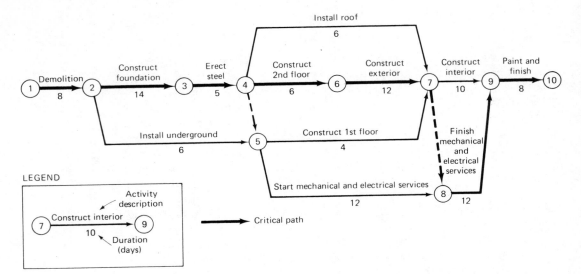

			Time (days)								
				Earliest		Latest		Float			
Start node (i)	End node (j)	Activity description	Duration	Start	Finish	Start	Finish	Total	Free	Independent	
*1	2	Demolition	8	0	8	0	8	0	0	0	
*2	3	Construct new foundation	14	8	22	8	22	0	0	0	
2	5	Install underground	6	8	14	27	33	19	13	13	
*3	4	Erect structure steel	5	22	27	22	27	0	0	0	
4	5	Dummy	0	27	27	33	33	6	0	0	
*4	6	Construct 2nd floor slab	6	27	33	27	33	0	0	0	
4	7	Install roof and refrigerator	6	27	33	39	45	12	12	12	
5	7	Construct 1st floor slab	4	27	31	41	45	14	14	8	
5	8	Start mechanical and electrical services	12	27	39	33	45	6	6	0	
*6	7	Construct exterior walls	12	33	45	33	45	0	0	0	
*7	8	Dummy	0	45	45	45	45	0	0	0	
7	9	Construct interior partitions	10	45	55	47	57	2	2	2	
*8	9	Finish mechanical and electrical services	12	45	57	45	57	0	0	0	
*9	10	Painting and finishing	8	57	65	57	65	0	0	0	

*Critical path.

Figure 5-12. (a) Network diagram; (b) Time schedule

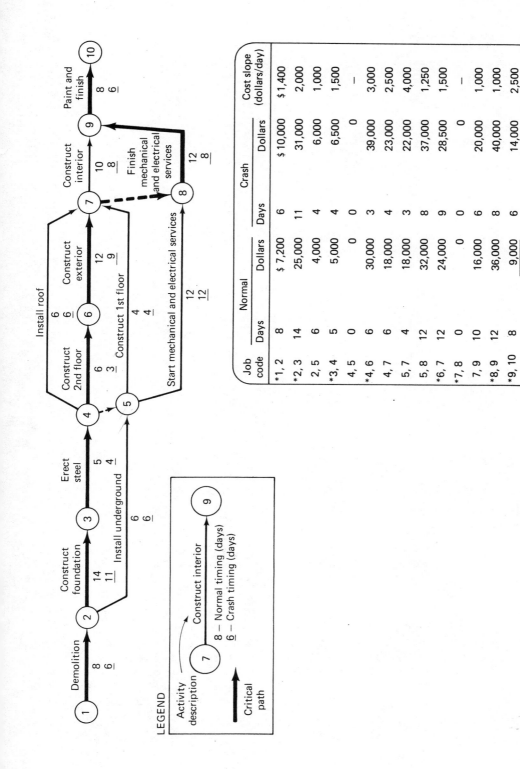

Job code	Normal		Crash		Cost slope (dollars/day)
	Days	Dollars	Days	Dollars	
*1, 2	8	$ 7,200	6	$ 10,000	$ 1,400
*2, 3	14	25,000	11	31,000	2,000
2, 5	6	4,000	4	6,000	1,000
*3, 4	5	5,000	4	6,500	1,500
4, 5	0	0	0	0	–
*4, 6	6	30,000	3	39,000	3,000
4, 7	6	18,000	4	23,000	2,500
5, 7	4	18,000	3	22,000	4,000
5, 8	12	32,000	8	37,000	1,250
*6, 7	12	24,000	9	28,500	1,500
*7, 8	0	0	0	0	–
7, 9	10	16,000	6	20,000	1,000
*8, 9	12	36,000	8	40,000	1,000
*9, 10	8	9,000	6	14,000	2,500
		$ 224,200			

*Critical path.

Figure 5–13. (a) Network diagram showing normal and crash times; (b) Normal crash data

85

Project duration (days)	Normal cost	Job code	Reduced time (days)	Additional cost	Normal and crash costs
65	$224,200	—	—	—	$224,200
63		8, 9	2	$2,000	226,200
61		1, 2	2	2,800	229,000
59		3, 4	1	1,500	
		6, 7	1	1,500	
			2	3,000	232,000
57		6, 7	2	3,000	235,000
55		2, 3	2	4,000	239,000
53		8, 9	2	2,000	
		7, 9	2	2,000	
			2	4,000	243,000
51		2, 3	1	2,000	
		9, 10	1	2,500	
			2	4,500	247,500
49		9, 10	1	2,500	
		4, 6	1	3,000	
			2	5,500	253,000
47		4, 6	2	6,000	259,000

Figure 5-14. Calculations of direct costs and total costs to crash the "Office Building Project"

Indirect costs consist of such items as overhead, insurance, interest on capitalization, production losses, and liquidated damage clauses. (Liquidated damages are paid to the owner if the project is not completed on time. Government contracts usually have this clause included.) Indirect costs have a tendency to decrease in cost with an increase in project duration. Tabulations for indirect costs for this example are shown in Figure 5-15.

In this example the cost slope of the indirect costs ($2,000/day) is greater than the weighted average of cost slopes of the direct costs (ranging from $1,000/day to $6,000/day). As a result, the total cost of this project is reduced as the duration time is reduced. The project duration can be "crashed" from 65 days to 57 days to reach the minimum cost. If time is a premium, the project can be "crashed" to its minimum duration time of 47 days. As the total project costs of $295,000 to perform work in 47 days is about the same as the budgeted

Project duration (days)	Direct costs	Indirect costs Normal	Indirect costs Crash	Indirect costs (normal and crash)	Total cost (direct and indirect)
65	$224,200	$70,000	—	$70,000	$294,200
63	226,200		$(4,000)	66,000	292,200
61	229,000		(4,000)	62,000	291,000
59	232,000		(4,000)	58,000	290,000
57	235,000		(4,000)	54,000	286,000
55	239,000		(4,000)	52,000	291,000
53	243,000		(4,000)	48,000	291,000
51	247,500		(4,000)	44,000	291,500
49	253,000		(4,000)	40,000	293,000
47	259,000		(4,000)	36,000	295,000

*Indirect cost slope: ($2,000 per day) — indirect costs include overhead, insurance, interest on capital loan, etc.

Figure 5-15. Calculations of additional indirect costs and total costs to crash the "Office Building Project"

$294,200 to perform work in 65 days, there was no cost penalty to expedite work. If minimum costs are important, the project can be completed in 57 days for $286,000, the lowest total project cost.

Figure 5-16 displays the total cost curve for the 47–65 day period, which shows clearly the optimum project duration time that falls somewhere between the normal time and the crash time when the total project costs (the sum of indirect and direct costs) are considered.

The last step in this procedure is to recalculate the project schedule once the revised job estimates are established for the new project duration time. This serves not only as a check but provides a new schedule once the revised job estimates are established for the new project duration time.

SUMMARY

Summarizing the cost-minimizing technique: It is used in conjunction with the network planning method to determine the optimum completion time of a project or to accelerate the completion of a project, where necessary, at minimum additional cost. The information provided is of great value to management in the initial scheduling of a project and in making adjustments when there is a delay in accomplishing specific parts of the work.

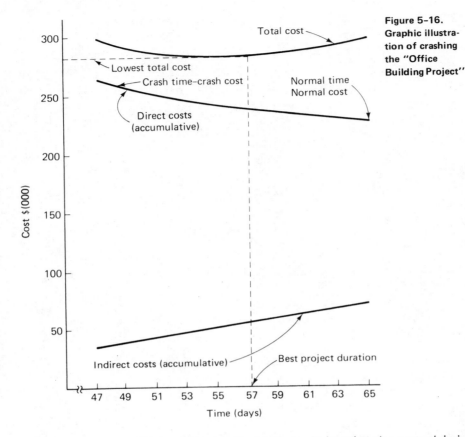

Figure 5–16.
Graphic illustration of crashing the "Office Building Project"

Two assumptions must be made in using the cost-minimizing procedure: Crash time is always less than or equal to normal time, and crash cost is always greater than or equal to normal cost. The procedure includes determining the direct cost, the indirect cost, and the total cost for the project in terms of the normal time and the crash time and the time intervals in between.

The cost-minimizing method can be applied manually for a small project; however, for a large project, a computer must be used if the work is to be done effectively. With the cost-minimizing computer program, the computer will make all the normal and crash time calculations and compute the minimum-cost curve. It will also print all the data required for scheduling the project, including earliest and latest start, earliest and latest finish, and float.

When used effectively with network planning, the cost-minimizing technique, whether done manually or with a computer program, provides management with an effective tool that can be used in planning and scheduling projects.

6

Resource Leveling

We have shown so far that through the proper use of the network analysis technique we can plan, schedule, and control projects with some degree of confidence. However, in following the project management cycle to this point, we have made one major assumption:

> There is no restriction on availability of labor,
> equipment, and/or other resources

In applications where labor or equipment limitations are not a restriction, the network planning technique can adequately deal with the planning, scheduling, and controlling of projects. However, in most situations there are labor and equipment shortages, and although enough labor may be available to complete the critical jobs on time, there may not always be enough workers to do all noncritical jobs in the time specified. Since the resource considerations are not inherent in network planning, but necessary for a proper planning and scheduling effort, the resource-leveling technique is used to produce a practical solution to the problem.

This is not a simple technique to apply. Planning the efficient use of resources is a complex task. One must not only effectively allocate resources among projects to meet scheduled target dates, but also select the most effective technical approach to the engineering and production work required for each project.

It is not unusual to have labor and equipment shortages. Physical restrictions, although not usually considered in the same light as availability limitations, can also be a major obstacle to straightforward scheduling. An example of a physical restriction is a confined location where only one person can work at a time; another example is a job that can be completed more safely or efficiently in daylight. Some of these limitations can be overcome if they are recognized in time. Where additional resources are needed, equipment can be rented, work may be contracted out, and for some projects, additional workers can be used on a part-time basis.

All of these alternatives add to the cost of the project. Therefore, it will be the planner's objective to minimize these additional costs.

Several definitions for resources are used in applying resource leveling. For our purposes, resources are limited to labor, equipment, facilities, and financial budgets. All of these factors must be considered when analyzing the duration of a project.

As labor is the main resource in most projects, our discussion will be directed to allocating labor. Therefore, our objective will be to apply the available resources within the prescribed project time limits. To achieve maximum efficiency within these parameters, an organization strives for the following goals:

1. Reduce the peaks and valleys in labor demands.

2. Minimize crew size.

3. Avoid idle or downtime.

4. Balance the overall labor requirements over reasonable periods of time.

Resource leveling also means resource stabilizing. Stabilizing your work force and achieving the goals listed above have the following advantages:

1. The main objective of any industry should be a consistent-project-life employee. Almost every organization wants employees to feel that once hired, they can be reasonably sure of consistent employment.

2. An organization wants to avoid layoffs and rehires. Not only is bringing workers in and out of a project costly and inefficient, but the peak demands are often difficult to meet.

3. There is another intangible inefficiency — workers "smell" the end of a job much better than supervisors can at times — and a subtle "slowdown" begins.

4. The situations described can exist not only in construction and industrial plants, but also in the technical and professional engineering fields.

The difficult part of solving the problem of resource leveling in the mathematical sense is usually the lack of any explicit criteria with which one can obtain the best use of resources. To establish a base, it will be necessary to arbitrarily establish available levels of resources as well as changes in levels. This situation exists to some degree in most of the organizations involved.

Techniques of Resource Leveling

In scheduling labor, whether for a large or a small project, to complete the project on time the highest priority for scheduling orders are the jobs on the critical path. Changing the scheduling of the critical jobs to adjust for leveling out labor is the last process. Therefore, the sequence to use in scheduling is as follows:

- Job with the least float
- Remaining noncritical jobs

In small jobs a manual leveling procedure can be used. When the project is large, computer programs are available that follow the same procedure as the manual approach to assist resource leveling purposes. Use of the computer will be discussed later in this chapter.

RESOURCE-LEVELING PROCEDURES

This procedure can be used after: first, defining the objectives; second, preparing a network diagram; and then, after preparing a schedule of the project, defining the critical and noncritical work items. The following steps should be completed:

Step 1. Plot all work items on a bar chart by early start times.

Step 2. Schedule all work items to start at their earliest start time if all required resources are available.

Step 3. If all required resources are not available, delay the start of each item until the resources are available within the float time of the specific work item.

Step 4. Make necessary scheduling adjustments in the following order:

- Noncritical jobs
- Jobs almost on the critical list
- Critical jobs

Step 5. If the start of a work item is delayed so much that it cannot be completed by its latest finish time and available float is exceeded, there are two options to level the available labor:

- Increase the resource limit for that activity.
- Schedule the start of the work items as soon as resources permit.

Step 6. If you cannot increase the resource limit and the start of work is to be delayed, you need to examine the effect on all work items dependent on it.

Step 7. When recomputing the network schedule, you must keep fixed the start and finish times of the work items already scheduled.

Step 8. Continue the process until all work items are scheduled.

RESOURCE ALLOCATION ILLUSTRATION:
Building Design Project[1]

To illustrate the manual method for labor scheduling, we consider the plan of an architectural engineering firm that is preparing a set of building designs and specifications.

Project Objectives

1. Complete the project in 8 weeks instead of the 9 weeks that were originally scheduled.

2. Maintain a constant crew size of six engineers.

From the network planning diagram in Figure 6–1, we know that Jobs A, D, F, and G are on the critical path, and since there is no float time, these jobs (with the possible exception of A) cannot change from a timing or labor stand-

[1] Adapted from Byron M. Radcliffe, Donald E. Kowal, and Ralph J. Stephenson, *Critical Path Textbook* (Chicago: Cahners Publishing Company, Inc., 1967), pp. 101-104.

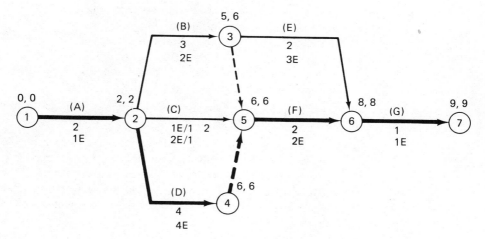

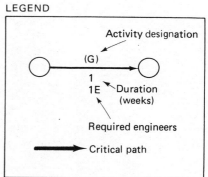

LEGEND

Job	Description	Latest finish	Earliest start	Duration (weeks)	Total float
1, 2 (A)	Preliminary design	2	0	2	0*
2, 3 (B)	Specification	6	2	3	1
2, 4 (D)	Building design	6	2	4	0*
2, 5 (C)	Site design	6	2	2	2
3, 6 (E)	Specification and proposal	8	5	2	1
5, 6 (F)	Review	8	6	2	0*
6, 7 (G)	Submit design and specification package	9	8	1	0*
4, 5	Dummy	6	6	0	0*
3, 5	Dummy	6	5	0	1

*Critical path items.

Figure 6–1. (a) Network diagram; (b) Total float tabulations

point. Therefore, our leveling tasks will deal with Jobs B, C, and E, which have float or optional starting and finishing times.

Our initial leveling efforts will follow this procedure:

- Draw a simple bar chart showing each job starting at its earliest start time and continuing for its assigned duration.

- Show the weekly (or whatever unit of time is being considered) crew on the bar chart. (See Figure 6-2.)

- Total the daily crew. In using the earliest start as a basis for the schedule, there is a variation in assignments, ranging from a maximum of eight engineers down to one engineer over the span of 9 weeks. This schedule also reflects poor work continuity, and the project completion time remains 9 weeks, which indicates that neither project objective has been used.

- By graphing the daily crew requirements, one can readily see the peaks and valleys of using the earliest start schedule. (See Figure 6-3.)

Drawing the chart by the graphical method is fairly simple. The horizontal scale represents the weeks (or whatever unit of time is being used), and the vertical scale represents the number of engineers (or whatever type of labor or skills that would be used.)

Each work item is drawn as a rectangle whose length represents the duration of the activity and the height is the number of personnel required for that job. The duration is taken from the bar chart.

Job	Working weeks									Total engineering weeks
	1	2	3	4	5	6	7	8	9	
A*	—1E—1E—									2
B			2E—2E—2E		→					6
C			1E—2E			→				3
D*			4E—4E—4E—4E							16
E						3E—3E		→		6
F*	LEGEND Float 2E						2E—2E			4
G*	Required engineers								1E	1
Total engineers	1	1	7	8	6	7	5	2	1	38

Figure 6-2. Labor leveling: bar chart time schedule (using earliest start time)

* Critical path.

Figure 6-3. Graphic load chart of labor allocation (using earliest start time)

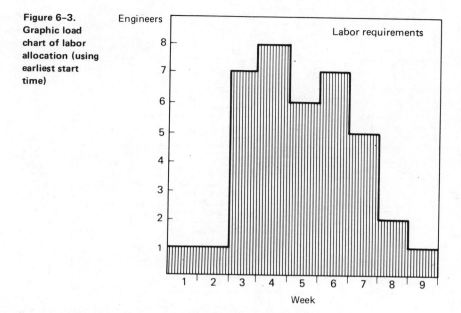

Showing both the bar chart schedule and the graphical representation on the same sheet has some decided advantages. It affords the opportunity to show the effect on the labor graph at the same time that adjustments are made on the bar chart time schedule.

Additional leveling efforts are required, as there exists poor work continuity and the work schedule has not been shortened. The next move is to reassign some of the float time from the noncritical jobs.

- The first step is a fairly simple approach. Adjust the bar chart time schedules to show the noncritical jobs starting at their *latest start* and continuing for its assigned duration.

- With all noncritical jobs starting at their latest start, check work force continuity and make the necessary adjustments.

- Through further adjustments within the range of the optional starting and finishing times, the time schedule is arranged. (There is one week during which the crew size will be more than the objective crew size of six engineers. If it is necessary to hold the six-engineer crew size, overtime or extending the project will be required. As the project date is apparently fixed, overtime for one or several work activities appears to be necessary.)

- To investigate the possibility of reducing the project duration, observe the jobs that can be reduced in time by doubling the crew size. In this case we were able to reduce the time of Job A by 1 day by doubling the number of workers. (In many cases, doubling the crew size would not necessarily cut the required time in half.)

Job	Working weeks 1	2	3	4	5	6	7	8	Total engineering weeks
A	2E								2
B		2E	2E		2E				6
C				2E	1E				3
D		4E	4E	4E	4E				16
E						3E	3E		6
F						2E	2E		4
G								1E	1
Total engineers	2	6	6	6	7	5	5	1	38

LEGEND

2E

Required engineers

**Figure 6-4.
Final labor level-
ing: adjusted
schedule**

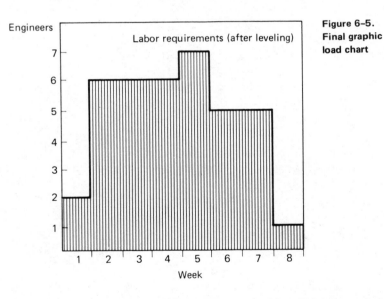

**Figure 6-5.
Final graphic
load chart**

Engineers

Labor requirements (after leveling)

Week

- The last step is to review the network diagram to see if the schedule changes made necessitate a change in the network plan.

(Figures 6-4 and 6-5 show the final schedule and graphical representation of leveling the labor in this example.)

This example is rather simple, and the analysis, if followed in the sequence that has been outlined, is not too difficult. This procedure can also be used for multiple resources; however, scheduling and resource allocation can become complex with larger and more involved projects. When this occurs, we resort to the computer. The use of the computer for assisting in resolving resource leveling situations is described in the remaining portion of this chapter.

RESOURCE LEVELING BY COMPUTER

Where the projects are large, a computer is employed to furnish the countless numbers of arithmetical and logical conclusions needed to make the resource-leveling decisions. There are a number of computer programs that are set up to meet resource-leveling needs. As these programs use the data from the network diagram input, the project must first be planned according to the procedure prescribed in network analysis.

RESOURCE ALLOCATION EXAMPLE – COMPUTER APPLICATION: BUILDING PROJECT

The building project network shown in Figure 6-6 will be used to illustrate resource leveling utilizing an available computer program.

Each activity has a time estimate associated with it. To complete these activities in the specified time, certain resources are assumed, and these resources must be specified and noted for each activity, as shown in Figure 6-6. For instance, it is indicated that it will take 5 days to complete Job 5,7, "Finish Floor Electrical." This is an estimate based on one laborer and three electricians doing the job. Note how the labor required to do each activity is shown on the diagram. (In this example, only those resources that are considered critical are shown on the diagram.)

Required Resource Levels

Resources other than labor, such as facilities and equipment, must also be specified. For example, if two carpenters, one millwright, four laborers, one operator, and a hoisting crane are needed to place the floor concrete in a specified amount of time, this information should be indicated on the network diagram and must be shown on data input cards of the network planning timing program. The time estimated to complete that activity will also be designated. How they are noted on the data input cards will be shown on the instructions of the specific program being used.

When the timing program is run on the computer, we get the regular output of earliest start, latest start, earliest finish, latest finish, and float times for each

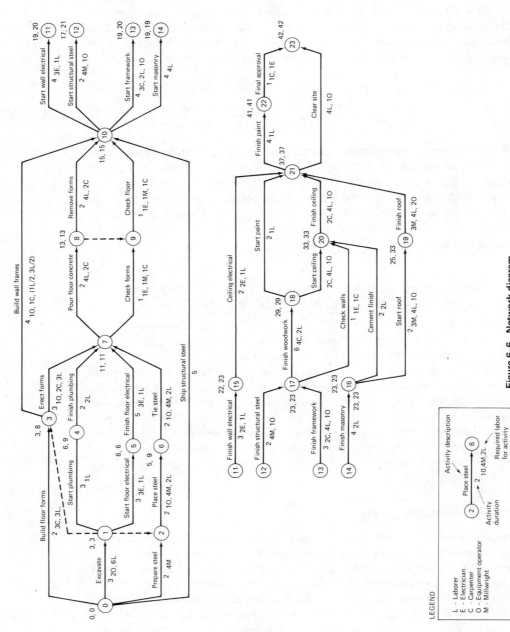

Figure 6-6. Network diagram

LEGEND

L – Laborer
E – Electrician
C – Carpenter
O – Equipment operator
M – Millwright

98

activity. This input for the sample problem is shown in Figure 6–7. The project completion time is 42 days. In the initial solution the resources were ignored, and thus 42 days is the normal project duration.

Resource-leveling Scheduling

In the first stage of resource leveling, the resources required by each time period, based on earliest start times, have been summarized by the computer. The avail-

i, j	Activity description	Time duration	Earliest Start	Earliest Finish	Latest Start	Latest Finish	Total	Free	Independent
0, 1	Excavate	3	0	3	0	3	0	0	0
0, 2	Prepare and reinforce steel	2	0	2	5	7	5	1	1
0, 3	Build floor forms	2	0	2	6	8	6	1	1
0, 10	Ship structural steel	5	0	5	10	15	10	10	10
1, 2	Dummy	0	3	3	7	7	4	0	0
1, 3	Dummy	0	3	3	8	8	5	0	0
1, 4	Start plumbing	3	3	6	6	9	3	0	0
1, 5	Start floor electrical	3	3	6	3	6	0	0	0
2, 6	Place and reinforce steel	2	3	5	7	9	4	0	0
3, 7	Erect forms	3	3	6	8	11	5	5	0
4, 7	Finish plumbing	2	6	8	9	11	3	3	0
5, 7	Finish floor electrical	5	6	11	6	11	0	0	0
6, 7	Tie and reinforce steel	2	5	7	9	11	4	4	0
3, 10	Build wall frames	4	3	7	11	15	8	8	3
7, 8	Place concrete floor	2	11	13	11	13	0	0	0
7, 9	Check forms	1	11	12	13	14	2	1	1
8, 9	Dummy	0	13	13	14	14	1	0	0
8, 10	Remove forms	2	13	15	13	15	0	0	0
15, 21	Ceiling electrical	2	22	24	35	37	13	13	12
16, 17	Dummy	0	23	23	23	23	0	0	0
16, 19	Start roof	2	23	25	31	33	8	0	0
16, 20	Cement finish	2	23	25	31	33	8	8	8
17, 18	Finish woodwork	6	23	29	23	29	0	0	0
18, 20	Start ceiling	4	29	33	29	33	0	0	0
17, 20	Check walls	1	23	24	32	33	9	9	9
18, 21	Start paint	2	29	31	35	37	6	6	6
19, 20	Dummy	0	25	25	33	33	8	8	0
19, 21	Finish roof	4	25	29	33	37	8	8	0
20, 21	Finish ceiling	4	33	37	33	37	0	0	0
21, 22	Finish paint	4	37	41	37	41	0	0	0
21, 23	Clear site	4	37	41	38	42	1	1	1
22, 23	Final approval	1	41	42	41	42	0	0	0

Figure 6-7. Schedule tabulation

ability of each resource for the project has also been given, period by period. (See Figure 6-8.) The computer will then attempt to schedule the jobs within the framework of the network planning solution so that available resources are not exceeded. Its approach is essentially the same as the manual method. Jobs with float will be deferred to beyond the "peak" requirement period.

Since most of the jobs require more than one craft, the decision of which jobs to start and which jobs to defer becomes complicated. Also, when a job is deferred, it potentially defers every other job in the project that follows it in a logical sequence. Without computer assistance, leveling would be a long and tedious task.

In following the same approach for leveling as the manual method, the computer is programmed for this sequence: assign the resources for those jobs on the critical path; assign float time; and schedule the remaining jobs with float time. The computer program is basically a trial-and-error process and the leveling is a function of the order of the input data cards. The input order should, therefore, normally reflect the relative importance of the jobs in the project.

In every case we have to assume that there are enough personnel available for work on the critical jobs, so critical jobs will be scheduled first. Noncritical jobs will then be scheduled with the resources that remain. If there are so many noncritical jobs that cannot be completed on time with the limited resources available, the project duration will need to be extended beyond the time predicted for completion by the original timing solution.

Once leveling has been completed, the next step is to compare the "leveled" resource requirements with the available resources and decide how best to distribute the resources to accomplish the project in the required time.

There may be projects where the available resources are not on a constant level throughout the project, and computer programs can usually accommodate

A — Architect	G — Pipe fitter	*O — Equipment operator
B — Bricklayer	*H — Heavy equipment	P — Plumber
*C — Carpenter	I — Ironworker	Q — Painter
D — Design engineer	J — Inspector	S — Table saw
*E — Electrician	*L — Laborer	T — Truck driver
F — Cement finisher	*M — Millwright	W — Welder

*Critical resources.

Summary of resource availability (constant levels)

Period	H	L	O	M	C	E
1–42	3	7	2	4	3	3

Figure 6–8. Labor and equipment identification for resource-leveling program

changes in availability of labor. Therefore, it will be necessary to specify the resource levels on a period-by-period basis, allowing for the levels of availability to be changed. This does allow some flexibility, since it is quite usual that several projects go on at the same time. By specifying the resource levels on a period-by-period basis, it is often possible to transfer resources from one project to another, which will result in efficient projects. The major benefit is that this will also tend to reduce project expenditures.

For this sample problem, a resource summary was requested after we ran the program calculating the timing schedule. The resource summary is shown in Figure 6-9. (Only the five critical trades and one critical equipment item are shown in the tabulation chart.) The time periods are listed down the page so that one can readily identify the resources needed at any particular time period. As discussed previously, the initial resource leveling effort will list all activities, starting at their earliest start times.

(For convenience, to show both the summary of resource requirements and resource availability, the computer printouts were reproduced, with some modification, in Figures 6-8 and 6-9.)

Most computer programs can provide a printout showing a graphical presentation (or resource chart) of resource requirements by plotting the type of

Period	H	L	O	M	C	E
1	5	9	2	4	3	0
2	5	9	2	4	3	0
3	5	6	1	0	0	0
4	4	10	4	4	4	3
5	4	10	4	4	4	3
6	2	8	4	4	3	3
7	1	6	2	4	1	3
8	0	3	0	0	0	3
9	0	1	0	0	0	3
10	0	1	0	0	0	3
11	0	1	0	0	0	3
12	2	4	2	2	2	1
36	0	4	1	0	2	0
37	0	4	1	0	2	0
38	3	5	1	0	0	0
39	3	5	1	0	0	0
40	3	5	1	0	0	0
41	3	5	1	0	0	0
42	0	0	0	0	1	1

Figure 6-9. Summary of resource requirements

resource against time. The resource chart for this sample problem is shown in Figure 6-10. Also plotted on the chart will be the resource availability.

The earliest start schedule shows that the resource requirements for carpenters, equipment operators, and laborers tend to exceed the available resources near the beginning of the project as well as showing great variations in peaks and valleys during the course of the project.

As the schedule worked out by initial computer solutions indicated that the project duration of 42 days cannot be contained within the available resources, it will be necessary for some of these jobs to be deferred beyond the "peak" period. For example, the resource summary calls for nine laborers the first day; but no matter how they are distributed, there are only seven laborers available.

A bar chart time schedule shown in Figure 6-11 reflects the initial computer solution. The project duration of 42 days is contained in this schedule; however, in specific periods, the labor requirements exceed the available carpenters, equipment operators, and laborers. Unless these trades can work overtime to keep the project within schedule, the duration needs to be extended.

Since most of the jobs require more than one trade, the decision of which jobs to start and which jobs to defer becomes complicated. Also, when a job is deferred, it potentially defers every other job in the project that follows it in a logical sequence.

(Few employers today are able to enjoy a union craft classification where

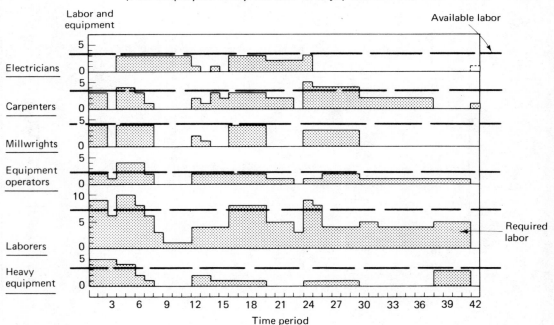

Figure 6-10. Labor availability and requirements: earliest start schedule

Activity		Time (days)	Schedule	
i, j	Description		Begin	End
0, 1	Excavate	3	0	3
0, 2	Prepare steel	2	0	2
0, 3	Build floor forms	2	0	2
0, 10	Ship structural steel	5	3	8
1, 4	Start plumbing	3	3	6
1, 5	Start floor electrical	3	3	6
1, 2	Dummy	0	3	3
1, 3	Dummy	0	3	3
3, 7	Erect forms	3	3	6
2, 6	Place steel	2	6	8
4, 7	Finish plumbing	2	6	8
5, 7	Finish floor electrical	5	6	11
3, 10	Build wall frames	4	8	12
17, 18	Finish woodwork	6	24	26
17, 20	Check walls	1	30	31
18, 20	Start ceiling	4	30	34
18, 21	Start paint	2	31	33
16, 19	Start roof	2	33	35
19, 20	Dummy	0	35	35
19, 21	Finish roof	4	35	39
20, 21	Finish ceiling	4	35	39
22, 23	Final approval	1	43	44*
21, 23	Clear site	4	39	43

*Project duration: 44 days.

Figure 6-11. Adjusted bar chart time schedule (after labor leveling)

one worker can be assigned to do any type of work. Consequently, resource requirements need to be considered by individual trades or classifications, and plotting total numbers of personnel has very little significance. Handling the individual crafts separately is required, because in most cases workers cannot be freely moved from one craft classification to another.)

In every case, we have to assume that there are enough personnel available for work on the critical jobs and period by period; critical jobs will therefore be scheduled first. Noncritical jobs will then be scheduled with the resources that remain. However, there may be so many noncritical jobs that cannot be completed on time with the limited resources available that the project duration would be extended beyond the time predicted for completion by the original timing solution.

For this sample problem we have established that some of the jobs must be deferred. The way this is most commonly done is to (1) do the jobs on the critical path; and (2) with any resources left over, do the jobs with the smallest total float time. The computer program is basically a trial-and-error process and the leveling is a function of the order of the input data cards. The input ordering should, therefore, normally reflect the relative importance of the jobs in the project.

If the required resources are unavailable when a critical job is scheduled to start, the start is delayed to the earliest time when adequate resources are available. This, of course, will lengthen the duration of the project.

From the solution some of the jobs that were not originally on the critical path may have become critical. A new schedule will be required to take into account the extended project duration date.

Project Duration (Revised)

By doing the jobs that are truly most critical at any given time, the resource leveling program was able to complete the sample problem in 44 days with constant levels of availability.

Although the 44-day duration is longer than the 42 days predicted by the original network planning solution, it is the shortest length of time in which this project can be done with the available labor and equipment. The time schedule tabulation based on the computer calculations for the 44-day schedule is shown in Figure 6-12.

The resource chart for the 44-day schedule is reproduced in Figure 6-13. This chart shows the success of the leveling effort of the computer program by superimposing the labor requirements based on the earliest start schedule.

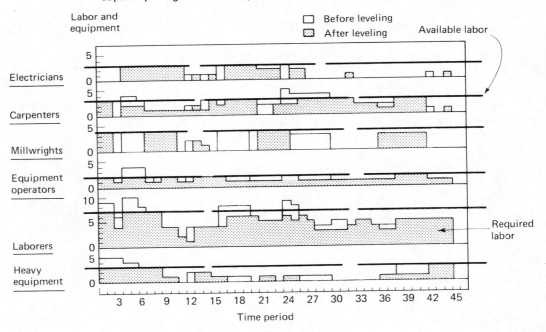

Figure 6-12. Time schedule tabulation (after leveling)

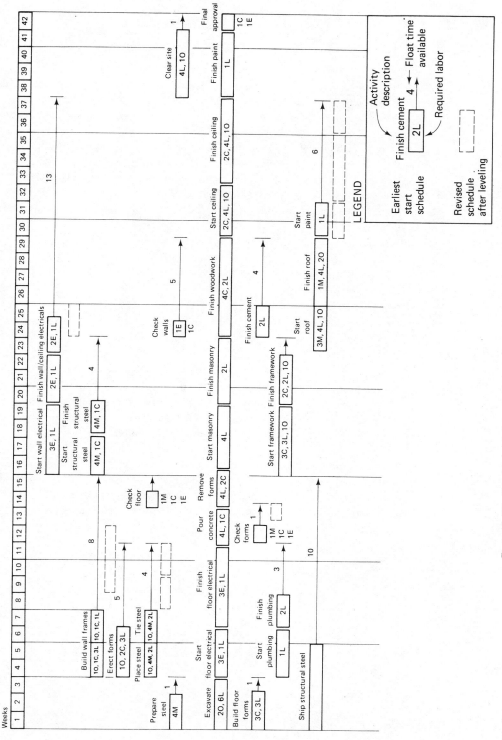

Figure 6-13. Graphic load chart of required and available labor (after labor leveling)

105

SUMMARY

A complete planning process needs to include time and cost factors which have to be satisfactorily related in the project schedule. An additional factor must be considered: the resources available to do the jobs, such as labor, equipment, space, and funds.

The resource-leveling program, whether by a manual approach if the project is small, or by using a computer program for longer projects, allocates the resources available for a project in such a manner that period-to-period changes in the levels of resources will be minimized. The resource-leveling program can also be used to determine a minimum project duration given a limited quantity of resources.

The leveling of resources involves these actions:

- The resource levels: the number of construction or industrial tradespeople, engineers, and programmers; the number and types of equipment required; and available funds are specified for each job.

- In the computer program, a printout will show the skills and equipment required by the time period (assuming that each job is to be scheduled at its earliest start time).

- With the availability of each resource given period by period, the computer then attempts to schedule the jobs and equipment within the framework of the planning network so that specified availabilities are not exceeded. If this is impossible, the program will extend the length of time of the project until a feasible schedule is obtained.

The resource-leveling program is a valuable tool for the project planner. The program can provide many answers to resource-leveling problems; however, the solution from resource leveling needs to be compared with other factors, such as cost, timing, and other management objectives before arriving at a desirable plan.

7

The Role of
the Computer

Project management is basically a method of planning and scheduling projects through the use of various "tools" that are available. One "tool" available that is of great value is the computer. The computer can take over some of the routine calculations and do them faster and with more accuracy. It *cannot analyze* or plan a project.

Previous chapters have included a description of the use of the network planning method in analyzing small projects. Network planning is also used in projects comprising thousands or tens of thousands of activities. When the project size exceeds 100 activities, it becomes desirable and, in many cases, necessary to use a digital computer to aid in performing the analysis.

In general, when a question arises on whether a computer is required in applying the network planning method to a project, the decision is made on the basis of the size and complexity of the project, the type of analysis desired, and the frequency that the network will be updated.

The size has a direct effect on the time required and cost incurred in using the computer for calculating the schedule. For example, the computer can perform timing calculations for a large project in minutes that might require days of manual calculations. Complexity is a factor because the more complicated the diagram is, the more difficult it is to perform calculations by hand accurately.

The type of analysis desired is a factor because even though simple timing calculations can be performed manually for a small project, time/cost trade-offs analysis and resource-leveling analysis require the use of a computer.

The frequence at which the project status is to be updated may also determine the need for using a computer. If frequent updating is desirable, it is often preferable to process the data through a computer, even for a small project.

For expediency in this book we will consider the computer as a "black box" that performs the mathematical and analytical calculations done by human beings but in a shorter length of time. Although we will not elaborate on how the black box functions, we believe that, to utilize the computer effectively, the student should develop a general feeling for the characteristics, ability, and "personality" of this black box.

Therefore, before showing how the computer can be used in planning, scheduling, and controlling projects, we will review briefly the physical elements of a computer, known as hardware, and computer programs that instruct the computer, known as software.

Computer Hardware

Computers vary tremendously in size and capability; however, its *hardware*, or physical equipment, operates as an integrated system. All the units are under the control of the central processor and will allow this basic layout:

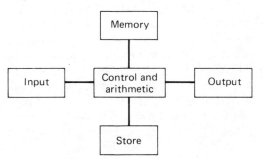

1. *Input* devices feed the computer with data. These devices include punched card readers, visual display terminals, and even links with other computers. Input devices may also be known as peripherals.

    One of the most common forms of input for the computer is the punched card. This is divided into either 80 or 96 columns, with the holes in the columns representing numbers or letters of the alphabet. These cards are read by optical methods or by "brushes" which detect the position on the holes and create the appropriate pulse. A typical card reader could read 1,000 cards or 80,000 characters per minute.

Paper tape, about 1 inch wide, can be similarly punched with holes to represent data. Once again, typical speeds could be in the order of 1,000 characters per second.

Special typefaces use magnetic inks which can be read by the input of a computer. Units have even been produced that can read handwriting.

2. *Storage and memory (data base)* is the file store of the computer—making vast amounts of information available to the processor in an unbelievably short time—measured in millionths of a second. The computer can look up information held on magnetic disks and can add to or erase information on the disks.

Disk stores may be divided into two categories: those with disks that can be interchanged and stored elsewhere, and those with disks that are fixed in the machine.

Magnetic tapes are another storage device. Magnetized spots on the tape represent information in a way similar to a conventional tape recorder. A normal-sized reel of magnetic tape holds about 15 million characters and can transfer at speeds of up to 400,000 characters per second.

At first sight, it might seem that both forms of storage, disk and tape, are equally suitable for input and output to the system. However, this is not so. For example, if you wanted to access some piece of information at the end of a tape, you would need to run the whole length of the tape to reach it. This could take several minutes — a very long time in the computer world. On a disk, however, you can access information wherever it appears, anywhere on the surface of the disk. This is known as random access, and normally takes about 1/50 of a second.

Both forms of storage have their advantages, depending on the system application.

3. The *central processor* performs all calculations, simple logic tasks, and all input and output to the system. The heart of the computer, it draws instructions one by one from the memory and puts into effect the corresponding machine operations. Connecting all the units of the system, it directs the transfer of information. The memory unit has a two fold purpose — to act as a temporary store for data, and to hold the program that directs the operations of the computer.

4. *Output* is where the results come out. Frequently, this is a printing device, but other units are available, including visual display and punched card units. In many systems, output is to a terminal computer which prints out the results of inquiries made of the central system. The output units are also known as peripherals.

Peripherals are devices that enhance a basic computer configuration, providing the system with varying degrees of sophistication. They include input, output, and auxiliary storage:

- Input devices are console keyboards, punched paper tape, punched cards, magnetic tape, and cassettes.

- Printed output units are carriage, serial, and line printers. The carriage printer is limited to 5 to 20 characters per second; the serial printer, 10 to 85 characters per second; and the line printers, 100 to over 1,000 lines per minute.

- Auxiliary storage devices (for maintaining and accessing master files) include magnetic ledger cards, magnetic tape, and magnetic disks.

Computer Software (Telling the Computer What to Do)

Before any computer can start work, it must be provided with detailed instructions. The process of translating a problem into instruction that the computer can understand and use is called *coding* or *programming*. These programs are called the *software* of the system.

Computers need instruction to perform even the simplest task. A set of instructions is called a *program*. Before preparing a program, the programmer makes a flowchart to show the sequence of operations similar to the simplified chart shown in Figure 7-1.

There are two types of "languages" used in programs: machine language and coded language. A *machine language* consists of numerical symbols that are unique to a given type of computer. This is the only language that the computer understands. Programs written in machine language are very detailed and extensive, requiring many hours of tedious work to write. Programs are written in special instruction codes called *languages*. There are now many of these languages.

In a *coded language*, each word of instruction represents several steps in machine language. In some instances, the coded language

**Figure 7-1.
Simple flowchart
for calculating a
worker's pay**

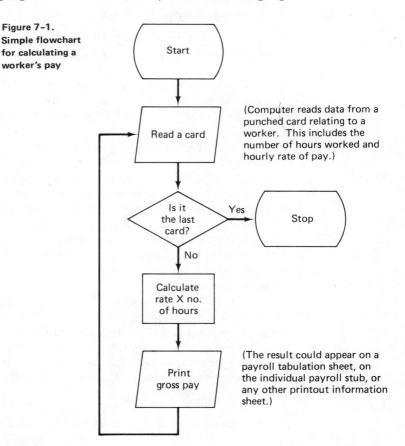

(Computer reads data from a punched card relating to a worker. This includes the number of hours worked and hourly rate of pay.)

(The result could appear on a payroll tabulation sheet, on the individual payroll stub, or any other printout information sheet.)

appears very similar to English, which the computer converts. A common coded language is FORTRAN(FORmula TRANslation). FORTRAN is a coded language that uses common scientific expressions and notations in its vocabulary. It is used primarily in scientific solutions. The most common language in business applications is COBOL (COmmon Business-Oriented Language).

COMPUTER APPLICATION

As we have discussed previously, the computer does not necessarily have to be used. The following factors will determine when a computer should be considered to be used:

- Size of the project
- Complexity of the project
- Type of analysis required
- Frequency the project needs to be updated

Size of the Project: A computer can do in minutes hand or manual calculations that may take days. Remember that the computer needs data input, and sometimes the nature of the input with its corrections can take a great deal of time, which could offset the time savings over manual methods.

Complexity: A complex program may be difficult to calculate manually. (However, time-consuming input data preparation can overshadow the benefits derived from computer calculations. You can get "bogged" down with the computer data sheets, also.)

Type of Analysis: Resource leveling and time/cost trade-offs, which contain a number of variables, can be done much more readily with a computer. When you need different sorts—categories by responsibility, float or early start, and so on—a computer wins "hands down."

Frequency: Once you get the "hang" of preparing the computer input as described for updating, you will normally find using a computer more desirable than making manual updates.

The use of the computer as a management "tool" in calculating schedules is evident when considering the factors listed above; and in project control, using the computer offers the following specific benefits:

- The reports can be structured in understandable, usable forms.

- Regular updating will require comparatively minimum personnel requirements.

- The time to produce updates and status reports is substantially reduced.

- Much manual effort, which is vulnerable to error is eliminated.

- Updating programs allows for added work activities to be inserted on others deleted with little effort at any stage during the course of the project.

COMPUTER PROGRAMS

There are well over 200 project management program packages available that have been prepared by computer firms to be used with their hardware system and by firms dealing in software packages only. Most of the programs are available through computer hardware equipment firms to users of their computer equipment. These programs are usually completely tested and ready for use, and consist of a program description, instruction manual, and a punched program card deck. Time and effort on the part of the user will still be necessary to acquire a working knowledge of the program package.

A representative list of computer program packages for project management applications currently available is as follows:

COMPUTER	PROGRAM NAME
*Honeywell	CPM-8
GE-115	Critical Path Method Program
*Honeywell	PMCS/66 Project Management and Control System
IBM 1130	PCS II — Project Control System
IBM Systems/360	PMS/360 — Project Management System
Univac 1107	Critical Path Analysis
	Project 2 — Boeing Computer Service, Inc.
	PMS Version IV — Project Management Systems, McDonald Douglas Automation Company

*Used by the author on a number of Ford Motor Company projects.

A typical software package will produce many types of reports including the following:

- *Scheduled Dates:* A time schedule of all work items that may be arranged in any number of sorts, such as earliest start, latest start, earliest finish, or latest finish dates. Schedules may also be sorted for total float time of each work item (and most programs can sort free and independent float times as well).

- *Bar Chart:* Shows graphically the calculated duration of the specified work items. Total float times and critical path are also shown.

- *Critical Activities:* A sorting of critical activities along paths of zero and low float times.

- *Milestones:* A listing of major events with their earliest finish (completion) dates. (Total float times can also be shown.)

- *Responsibility:* A sorting of work items according to the participating group responsible for their completion.

- *Resource Allocation:* A listing by each resource required for a given time span.

- *Resource Leveling:* A graphical representation of the daily resource usage within the scheduled resource requirements.

- *Project Costs:* A listing of the specified work items, together with the estimated total cost and the actual cost to date of each.

- *Cash Flow Schedules:* A listing of the specified work items, together with the estimated total cost and the actual cost to date for each, by calendar month.

- *Scheduled Earnings:* A listing of the cost status for all specified work items, showing estimated cost, projected cost, and actual cost to date.

- *Cost Optimization:* A time schedule of the work items that allows the project's duration to be shortened at minimum additional cost.

- *Work Status and Programs:* A listing of the specified work items with their scheduled early start and late finish dates, their remaining durations, and their preceding work items.

These reports represent only part of the basic information that a typical software package of a project management and content system can provide. The reports are designed to be incorporated in whatever format is best suited for each level of management, as well as for project supervision and analysts and financial analysts.

Computer manufacturers not only have additional programs but have made revisions and additional improvements to existing programs. Cost for these programs will vary, and details for purchase or lease should be discussed with the computer manufacturer.

· In addition to standard reports, there are patented software programs that produce project management graphical reports. Time-phased network diagrams can be plotted which display the flow of project activities and the overall impact of scheduling changes. Graphical reports can also include time-phased bar charts for reporting and monitoring schedule progress, as well as a wide variety of cost/resource graphs (cost, personnel requirements) used for budget and labor controls.

A sample program, "Computer Installation Project," will be used to illustrate the manner in which a computer is applied in the project management cycle of planning, scheduling, and controlling.

SAMPLE PROGRAM: COMPUTER INSTALLATION PROJECT

A flowchart depicting the steps in planning a project with the network planning method using the computer as a tool is shown in Figure 7–2.

Planning

Once the objectives have been established, the first step in the computer installation project consists of planning what is to be done.

Determining the Jobs Required

Proper listing of every step required to accomplish the project is of great importance. It is vital that all phases of work be encompassed by the jobs listed. Any omissions will cause inaccuracies in scheduling and may result in failure to complete the project on time.

Figure 7-3 lists the major phases of work involved in the computer project. These job descriptions should be phased in such a way that they:

1. State basic functions that can be understood by all concerned with managing the planning, scheduling, and control of the project.

2. Include all the work required in the project.

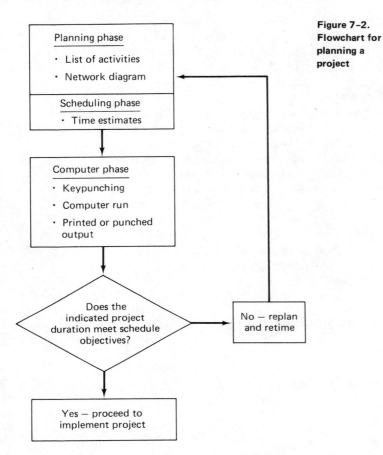

**Figure 7-2.
Flowchart for
planning a
project**

After the list of activities is completed, a network diagram (Figure 7-4) is prepared, showing the interrelations between the activities in the project.

Each job is identified by a node consisting of a circle and a number at the beginning and end of the arrow. "Decide on Computer" is specified as "Job 1,2." The numbers may be arranged in ascending order from 1 through 14 to aid in following the progress of the project.

In examining the diagram one sees:

1. "Decide on Computer" (1,2) must be completed before:
   a. "Determine Site Specification," because these specifications would be determined in part by the type of computer purchased.
   b. "Select Operating Personnel" and "Select Programming Personnel," because the qualifications required would be dependent to some extent on the type of computer.

The Ford Motor Company has been installing medium-scale computers for production control functions and this sample problem is a condensed version of the steps required to lay out the program for the installation. The objective is to make the computer system operational as soon as possible.

1. Decide on computer: Select computer configurations which will best fulfill needs.

2. Procure computer: Includes placing order for selected computer, fabricating, and delivery time.

3. Install computer: Physically install computer and related software.

4. Determine site specifications: Define physical environment for computer, including location, area size, environment requirements.

5. Solicit bids for site preparation: Contact appropriate contractors for bids, giving time frame requirements.

6. Award contract for site preparation: Award contract based on specifications and proposal price.

7. Prepare site: Design and build computer enclosure including environmental requirements.

8. Select programming personnel: Interview and select personnel based on education and experience; within project budget requirements.

9. Train programming personnel: Train for particular needs of project using the selected computer, and applying system standards of the company.

10. Select operating personnel: Interview and select personnel based on experience as an operator and with the selected computer within project budget requirements.

11. Train operating personnel: Train on computer system and on operating procedures of the company.

12. Layout computer records: Define and design files to fit the needs of the system.

13. Develop computer program: Design system appropriate for computer; code and test programs.

14. Test computer program: Test all programs run-to-run for continuity and balance back to manual controls.

15. Design forms: Define form needs and evaluate usage.

16. Procure forms: Order forms from appropriate outlet, giving volume requirements and needed date of receipt.

17. Put program into operation: Complete computer and user documentation, train users, communication for ongoing maintenance.

Figure 7–3. List of activities for the "Computer Installation Project"

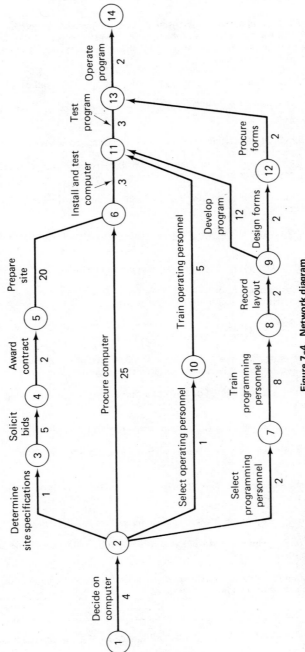

Figure 7–4. Network diagram

2. Several jobs can be accomplished concurrently. For example:
   a. "Determine Site Specifications" (2,3).
   b. "Procure Computer" (2,6).
   c. "Select and Train Operation and Programming Personnel" (2,10), (10,11), (2,7), (7,8).

3. "Test Program" can be strated only after the completion of:
   a. "Install and Test Computer" (6,11).
   b. "Train Personnel (Operating and Programming)" (7,8), (10,11).
   c. "Record Layout" (8,9).
   d. "Develop Program" (9,11).

In other words, the program cannot be tested until trained personnel have a program prepared and a computer that is operating.

Note that there is nothing unique about arrow diagramming; different people planning the same operation could come up with different plans and, therefore, different diagrams.

Some of the sequences of jobs are fairly rigid; it is very difficult to replace them with any other satisfactory sequence. An example is the series of jobs shown on the network diagram beginning with "Determine Site Specifications" and continuing through "Prepare Site." Each job must be completed before the succeeding job can be accomplished.

For other jobs, the sequence may vary depending on who is planning the project. The programming sequence illustrates this.

One person might decide that the "Develop Program" (9,11) needs to be completed before the "Record Layout" (8,9) is accomplished; another, that these two jobs could be simultaneous. Alternative sequences might also be used for "Design Forms" (9,12) — because the program may be changed, or it might be accomplished before developing the program if there is a long lead on securing the forms, which is normally the case. Regardless of how the plan is set forth in the arrow diagram, it provides an effective graphic display of what is planned to be done.

When the network diagram is approved, time estimates are made for each job and are shown beneath each job arrow. The planning of the work sequence and the estimating of job times at this stage are made on a normal time basis. The length of the project has not yet been determined. No effort is exerted at this point to compress the project duration or meet any particular deadline. If the output indicates that the project duration does not meet objectives, it will be necessary to replan the project and reduce some job times through expediting. At this point, simulation studies of alternative plans may require crash time/cost information for selected jobs to perform a time/cost compression analysis; and resource-leveling exercises may also be done.

SCHEDULING

The plan shown on the arrow diagram can also be presented for preliminary review without reference to timing. After approval of the job sequences is secured, the time estimates for accomplishing each job can be obtained.

The time estimate figures are shown below the arrows on the network diagrams: for example,

$$\xrightarrow{\text{Decide on Computer}} \quad ; \quad \xrightarrow{\text{Determine Site Specifications}}$$
$$\qquad\quad 4 \qquad\qquad\qquad\qquad\qquad\qquad 1$$

With a diagram of this size it is fairly simple, and the calculations for earliest start, latest finish, and total float can be done manually.

Computer Output — Scheduling Data

For large diagrams, the relations between jobs or activities are not so obvious, particularly if it is necessary to go through every possible path and compute the time factors. If hundreds of jobs are involved, the computations become very tedious and time consuming. For projects of this size, the computer is used.

The required input information is fed into the computer on a standard computer card, one job per card as follows:

- i,j: The i,j symbols are merely a sequence designation. Each arrow has a node at the beginning and end. The i,j for "Decide on Computer" is identified by nodes 1,2. The nodes indicate the location of the arrow (and job) in the diagram.

- Job Description: A brief phrase that describes the work to be done.

- Job Time: The estimated time for completing each job.

These data are placed into a format and then punched into a set of standard computer cards to make up a *data deck*. The format for punching the cards is determined by the computer program that will be used. An illustration of one particular format is shown on the data sheet in Figure 7–5, which applies to the computer installation project. (The explanation of this data sheet begins on page 115.) It should be emphasized that this format corresponds to only one particular computer program.

The information to be punched is first written on the data sheet, one character to a column. Certain columns must contain numeric

Figure 7-5. Data input sheet

Data sheet (card columns 1–80, with an **Identification** field in columns 73–80)

Calendar / week scale (top of sheet):

	Dates across the weeks
WEEKS	1 … 40/1 … 52
Row 2	JAN 6, JAN 13, JAN 20, JAN 27, FEB 3, FEB 10, FEB 17, FEB 24, MAR 2, MAR 9, MAR 16, MAR 23
Row 3	MAR 30, APR 6, APR 13, APR 20, APR 27, MAY 4, MAY 11, MAY 18, MAY 25, JUN 1, JUN 8, JUN 15
Row 4	JUN 22, JUN 29, JUL 6, JUL 13, JUL 20, JUL 27, AUG 3, AUG 10, AUG 17, AUG 24, AUG 31, SEP 7
Row 5	SEP 14, SEP 21, SEP 28, OCT 1 …

Column-position guide (row 7): 1 2 3 4 5 6 7 8 9 0 1 2 3 4 5 6 7 8 9 0 1 2 3 4 5 6 7 8 9 0 1 2 3 3 3 3 3 3 4 4 4 4 4 4 4 5 5 5

SAMPLE PROBLEM

1 – COMPUTER INSTALLATION   0 DEC 20 6300 1   5 1300 1   4

No.	Activity	Dept	Duration
2	DECIDE ON COMPUTER	MGT	1
3	DETERMINE SITE SPECS	SYS	25
6	PROCURE COMPUTER	PUR	2
7	SELECT PROGRAMMING PERSONNEL	PER	1
10	SELECT OPERATING PERSONNEL	MGT	5
4	SOLICIT BIDS	PUR	2
5	AWARD CONTRACT	MGT	20
6	PREPARE SITE	SUB	3
11	INSTALL AND TEST COMPUTER	MFG	8
8	TRAIN PROGRAMMING PERSONNEL	TRN	2
9	DESIGN RECORD LAYOUT	PROG	12
12	DEVELOP PROGRAM	PROG	2
9	DESIGN FORMS	SYS	5
11	TRAIN OPERATING PERSONNEL	TRN	3
13	TEST PROGRAM	PROG	8
13	PROCURE FORMS	PUR	2
14	OPERATIONAL PROGRAM TEST	OPER	
	END OF PROJECT		

characters only; other columns may contain either numeric or alphabetic characters. The particular computer program to be used determines the required format. Violations of the format will cause the program to reject the input data.

Each line on the data sheets represents one punched card. When complete, the data sheets are turned over to a keypunch operator (or to anyone who has completed keypunching training) for punching into cards. Keypunching can also be done by outside keypunching services or there may be in-house keypunching operations.

Punched Card Code System

The punched card code for representing letters, numbers, and special characters is illustrated in Figure 7-6. The samples shown also illustrate elements of the punched card, such as the 12 punching positions, zone punches, numeric punches, a card column, and a card row. The keypunch operator types the punched cards in a manner similar in some aspects to the operation of a regular typewriter. The keyboard has letters, numbers, and characters which are, for the most part, in the same position as on a regular typewriter. The keypunch has uppercase letters only and some special characters that are not included on a regular typewriter.

EXAMPLE OF DATA CARDS

The information that is put on the data sheet for keypunching is determined by the type of analysis to be performed and the program to be used. The following material is an example of the information and format required by a particular project management computer program. This format may not be applicable to other computer programs or to a future revision of this program.

Six types of cards are punched from the data sheet for a standard timing analysis of the computer installation project. These cards have been punched from the data sheet and Figures 7-7 and 7-8 explain the meaning of the code characters on the cards. Each character must, of course, be punched in the exact column shown on the data sheet in order to be used by the program designed for this particular format.

Control Card: The control card (Figure 7-7) contains information on the options to be executed in processing the data deck. For example, codes on the card indicate whether the user wishes to substitute dates for the earliest start times and latest finish times;

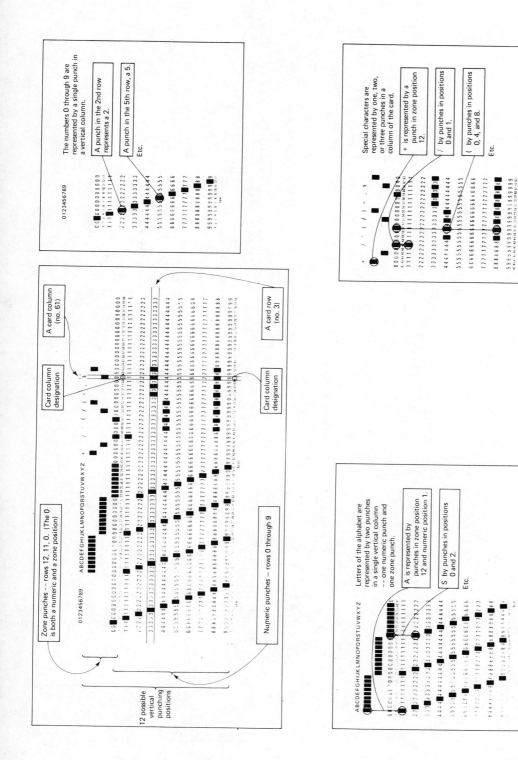

Figure 7-6. Recording numbers, letters, and special characters

123

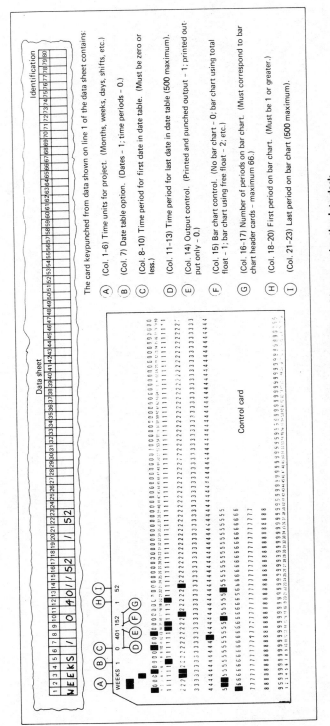
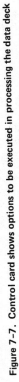

The card keypunched from data shown on line 1 of the data sheet contains:

(A) (Col. 1-6) Time units for project. (Months, weeks, days, shifts, etc.)

(B) (Col. 7) Date table option. (Dates – 1; time periods – 0.)

(C) (Col. 8-10) Time period for first date in date table. (Must be zero or less.)

(D) (Col. 11-13) Time period for last date in date table (500 maximum).

(E) (Col. 14) Output control. (Printed and punched output – 1; printed output only – 0.)

(F) (Col. 15) Bar chart control. (No bar chart – 0; bar chart using total float – 1; bar chart using free float – 2; etc.)

(G) (Col. 16-17) Number of periods on bar chart. (Must correspond to bar chart header cards - maximum 66.)

(H) (Col. 18-20) First period on bar chart. (Must be 1 or greater.)

(I) (Col. 21-23) Last period on bar chart (500 maximum).

Figure 7-7. Control card shows options to be executed in processing the data deck

124

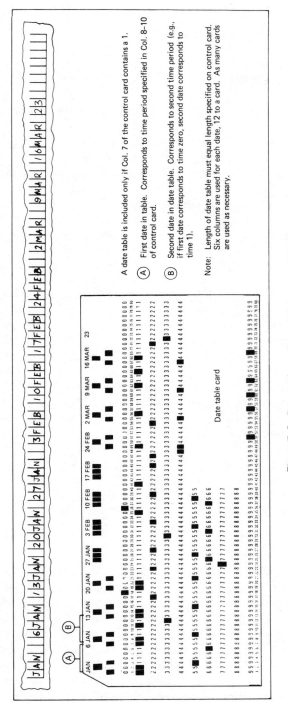

A date table is included only if Col. 7 of the control card contains a 1.

(A) First date in table. Corresponds to time period specified in Col. 8-10 of control card.

(B) Second date in date table. Corresponds to second time period (e.g., if first date corresponds to time zero, second date corresponds to time 1).

Note: Length of date table must equal length specified on control card. Six columns are used for each date, 12 to a card. As many cards are used as necessary.

Figure 7-8. Data table card shows dates to be included

125

whether a bar chart is to be printed; what periods the bar chart is to cover; and the heading for the bar chart.

Date Table Card: If the user elects to use a date table, cards containing the dates must be included (Figure 7–8).

Bar Chart Header Cards: When a bar chart is to be produced, bar chart header cards (Figure 7–9) provide a heading for the printed output.

Title Card: A title card (Figure 7–10) is required in the data deck to provide the project title, run number, and run date. The information on the title card will be printed on each sheet of output.

Activity Card: An activity card (Figure 7–11) is punched for each activity in the project. Activity cards for the basic timing analysis contain the *i*-node and *j*-node identification, the activity description, and the time duration of the activity. A code number indicating the responsibility for the activity and a cost estimate for the activity may also be included. When a time/cost estimate is to be performed, there will be additional cards that contain crash time and cost slope with their *i*-node and *j*-node designation. When resource-leveling analysis is to be performed, other activity cards will show the numbers and types of resources required for that activity. There will be additional cards showing resource availability. Dummy activities are treated in the same manner; the duration of a dummy activity is zero.

End-of-Project Card: The final card in the data deck is an end-of-project card (Figure 7–12). Several projects may be stacked in a single run. The end-of-project card for each project except the last will contain an "8" in column 1; the last will contain a "9" in column 1.

After receiving the punched cards (or data deck) from keypunching, obtain a listing. This listing is a computer run that duplicates the punched cards, which is to be compared with the initial data input sheets for errors, omissions, sequence of cards, and so on.

Program Deck

For the data deck to be processed, it is necessary to give the computer a complete set of instructions detailing each step in the analysis to be performed. This is known as the computer program.

Programs are originally written in an algebraic language and are translated into machine language by the computer, using a master program called a *compiler.* The machine language program is punched in binary form into a deck of cards, and it is this deck of punched cards that is fed into the computer as the program deck. Two decks are required to run a critical path project: the program deck and the data deck.

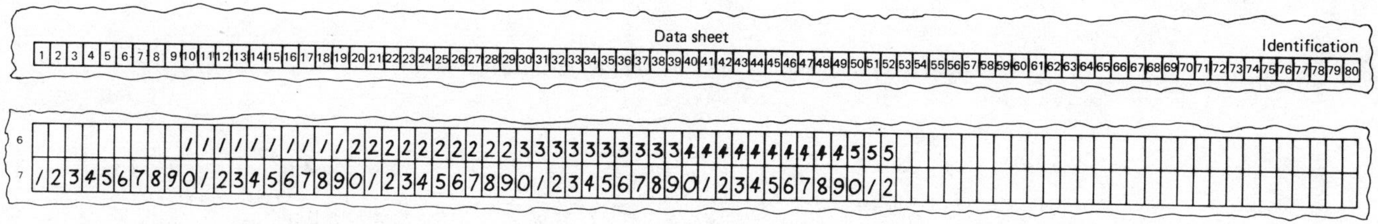

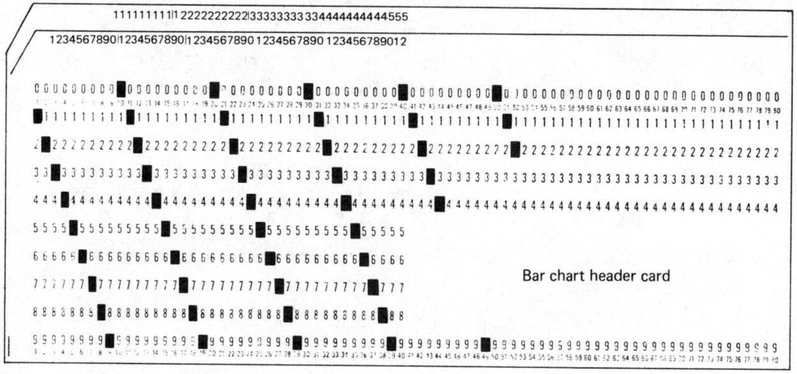

Figure 7-9. Bar chart header card provides a heading for the printed output

Two cards are always used. The sample cards shown represent the heading for a 52-week bar chart which corresponds to the length specified in Col. 16-17 of the control card. Other configurations may be used to represent up to a maximum of 62 time periods.

127

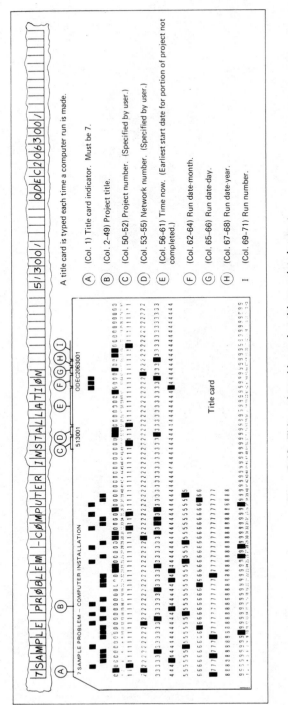

A title card is typed each time a computer run is made.

(A) (Col. 1) Title card indicator. Must be 7.

(B) (Col. 2-49) Project title.

(C) (Col. 50-52) Project number. (Specified by user.)

(D) (Col. 53-55) Network number. (Specified by user.)

(E) (Col. 56-61) Time now. (Earliest start date for portion of project not completed.)

(F) (Col. 62-64) Run date-month.

(G) (Col. 65-66) Run date-day.

(H) (Col. 67-68) Run date-year.

I (Col. 69-71) Run number.

Figure 7–10. Title card provides project title on printed output

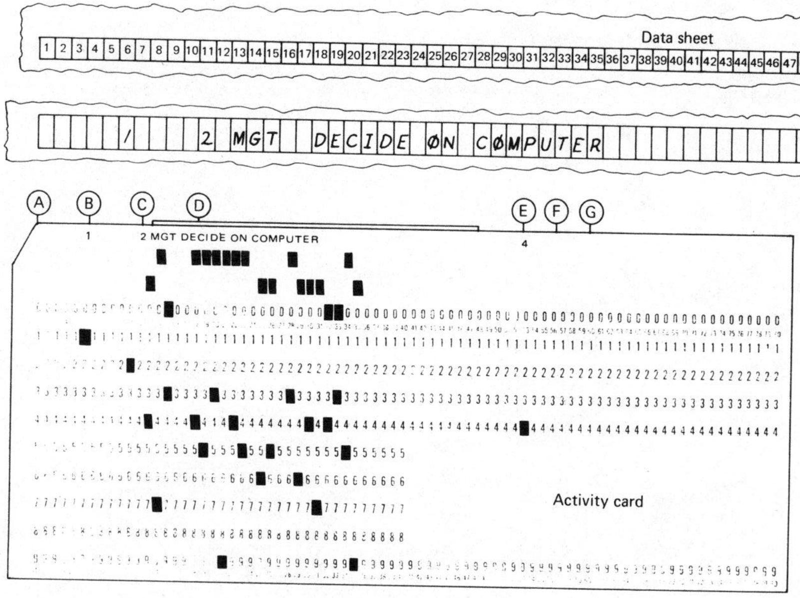

Figure 7-11. Activity card containing node designation, description of activity, and time duration

A — (Col. 1) Status code. (Unstarted activity – blank; in-progress activity –1; completed activity –3.)

B — (Col. 3–6) i node.

C — (Col. 8–11) j node.

D — (Col. 13–48) Activity description. (Part of description field may be used for a responsibility node, such as MGT used in this example.)

E — (Col. 50–53) Activity duration.

(Total activity time for unstarted activities; remaining activity time for in-progress activities.)

F — (Col. 55–60) Actual start date for in-progress and completed activities.

G — (Col. 61–66) Actual completion date for completed activities.

Note: For activity card shown, status code is blank, indicating activity is unstarted. Thus, actual start and completion dates are left blank.

129

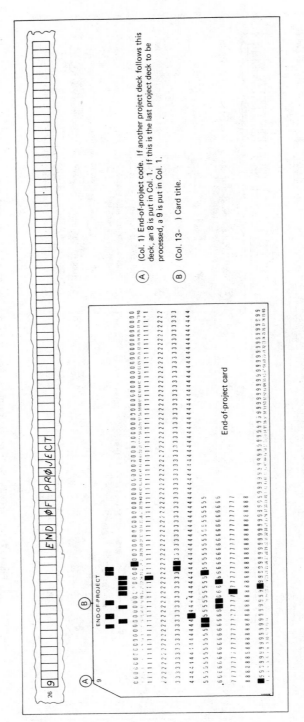

(A) (Col. 1) End-of-project code. If another project deck follows this deck, an 8 is put in Col. 1. If this is the last project deck to be processed, a 9 is put in Col. 1.

(B) (Col. 13-) Card title.

Figure 7-12. End-of-project card

The computer used must be the type on which the program was originally compiled. Project management programs generally require a large-scale computer.

THE COMPUTER

At the computer center, the total input decks—the program deck and the data deck—are read onto magnetic tape. (See Figure 7-13.) Next, the program portion is read from magnetic tape. The instructions in the program then take over and cause the computer to read the data deck from magnetic tape, store the data in specified areas of core storage, process the data, and store the results in other specified areas of core storage. When the processing is completed, further instructions in the program cause the results to be taken from core storage and put on another magnetic tape in the output format specified in the instructions. In many locations, this magnetic tape is removed from the large computer and taken to a smaller computer,

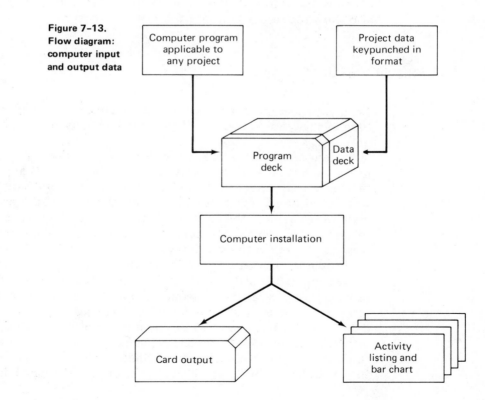

**Figure 7-13.
Flow diagram:
computer input
and output data**

where the information on the magnetic tape is printed. Any information that the program caused to be put on tape to be punched is also punched through the use of the smaller computer. The smaller computer, which is less expensive to operate, is used for the time-consuming input/output operations, which do not require large memory capacities.

Printed Output

Several kinds of output can be produced, including a listing of the jobs in the project, showing the earliest start time, latest finish time, and the float for each activity can be printed. A bar chart showing each job and the earliest and latest times at which it may be scheduled can also be printed. Sample printed output sheets for the computer installation project are shown in Figures 7–14 and 7–15. The first is a listing of the basic output data for the program; the second is a bar chart using total float.

The printout is checked to see if the scheduled objectives can be met. The float sort is generally used initially, as it can show any discrepancies more readily. The sample basic output data sheet can also show the responsible group for each activity.

ANALYSIS OF RESULTS

Normally, you are unable to use the first printout. Replanning with time changes are necessary, added activities may be required, and so on.

The user will be interested in determining whether the indicated project duration is satisfactory and whether it meets any deadlines that have been imposed. If the project duration is not satisfactory, it will be necessary to return to the initial phase of the critical path method, reevaluate the time requirements of jobs on the critical path to determine which of them can be reduced most readily, and, perhaps, to replan the way in which the work will be done in order to shorten the critical path and meet the deadline requirements.

Having replanned the diagram and reevaluated the times, the user will want to make a second computer run before initiating the project. The data deck is updated by removing those cards for which data have changed, and inserting new cards containing corrected information. It is likely that in replanning and retiming a job, only a small part of the network, comprising for the most part activities on the critical path, will have changed. Most of the original data deck is

PROJ. NO. 513   NETWORK NO. 001   TIME NOW 0

RUN DATE DEC 20   RUN NO. 001   PAGE NO. 1

PROJECT DURATION 40 WEEKS

S T I NODE	J NODE	ACTIVITY DESCRIPTION AND IDENTIFICATION	DURATION ESTIMATE	START EARLIEST	START REQD	COMPLETION EXPD	COMPLETION REQD	M I	TOTL	FREE	INDP	COST
1	2 MGT	DECIDE ON COMPUTER	4	JAN 6	JAN 6	FEB 3	FEB 3		0	0	0	0
2	3 SYS	DETERMINE SITE SPECS	1	FEB 3	FEB 3	FEB 10	FEB 10		0	0	0	0
2	6 PUR	PROCURE COMPUTER	25	FEB 3	FEB 24	JUL 17	AUG 17		3	3	3	0
2	7 PER	SELECT PROGRAMMING PERSONNEL	2	FEB 3	MAR 23	FEB 17	APR 6		7	7	0	0
3	10 MGT	SELECT OPERATING PERSONNEL	1	FEB 3	JUL 27	FEB 10	AUG 3		25	0	0	0
3	4 PUR	SOLICIT BIDS	5	FEB 10	FEB 10	MAR 16	MAR 16		0	0	0	0
4	5 MGT	AWARD CONTRACT	2	MAR 16	MAR 16	MAR 30	MAR 30		0	0	0	0
5	6 SUB	PREPARE SITE	20	MAR 30	MAR 30	AUG 17	AUG 17		0	0	0	0
6	11 MFG	INSTALL AND TEST COMPUTER	3	AUG 17	AUG 17	SEP 7	SEP 7		0	0	0	0
7	8 TRN	TRAIN PROGRAMMING PERSONNEL	8	FEB 17	APR 6	APR 13	JUN 1		7	7	7	0
8	9 PROG	RCD LAYOUT	2	APR 13	JUN 1	APR 27	JUN 15		7	7	7	0
9	11 PROG	DEVELOP PROGRAM	12	APR 27	JUN 15	JUL 20	SEP 7		7	7	0	0
9	12 SYS	DESIGN FORMS	2	APR 27	JUL 20	MAY 11	AUG 3		12	0	0	0
10	11 TRN	TRAIN OPERATING PERSONNEL	5	FEB 10	AUG 3	MAR 16	SEP 7		25	25	0	0
11	13 PROG	TEST PROGRAM	3	SEP 7	SEP 7	SEP 28	SEP 28		0	0	0	0
12	13 PUR	PROCURE FORMS	8	MAY 11	AUG 3	JUL 6	SEP 28		12	12	0	0
13	14 OPER	PROGRAM OPERATIONAL	2	SEP 28	SEP 28	OCT 12	OCT 12		0	0	0	0

TOTAL COST $ 0

Figure 7-14. Printed output schedule: data sheets

BAR CHART   PROJ. NO. 513   NETWORK NO. 001   TIME NOW   0

                   RUN DATE DEC 20   63 RUN NO.   001   PAGE NO.   1

USING TOTAL FLOAT

```
                                                           1ST  52 WEEKS
                                        111111111122222222223333333333444444444 4555
 I    J                         FLOAT  TIME  123456789012345678901234567890123456789012345678901 2
NODE  NODE  ACTIVITY DESCRIPTION        EST.
            AND IDENTIFICATION
  1   2 MGT  DECIDE ON COMPUTER            0    4  CCCC----------------------------------------------
  2   3 SYS  DETERMINE SITE SPECS          0    1  ----C---------------------------------------------
  2   6 PUR  PROCURE COMPUTER              3   25  ---XXCCCCCCCCCCCCCCCCCCCCCCCCC***-----------------
  2   7 PER  SELECT PROGRAMMING PERSONNEL  7    2  --XX---**-----------------------------------------
  2  10 MGT  SELECT OPERATING PERSONNEL   25    1  --X------------------*----------------------------
  3   4 PUR. SOLICIT BIDS                  0    5  ----CCCCC-----------------------------------------
  4   5 MGT  AWARD CONTRACT                0    2  ---------CC---------------------------------------
  5   6 SUB  PREPARE SITE                  0   20  -----CCCCCCCCCCCCCCCCCCCC-------------------------
  5  11 MFG  INSTALL AND TEST COMPUTER     0    3  -------------------------CCC----------------------
  6   8 TRN  TRAIN PROGRAMMING PERSONNEL   7    8  -----XXXXXXXC*******-----------------------------
  7   9 PROG  RCD LAYOUT                   7    2  ------XX------**---------------------------------
  8   9 PROG  DEVELOP PROGRAM              7   12  -------XXXXXXXCCCC*******-------------------------
  9  12 SYS  DESIGN FORMS                 12    2  ----------XX------**-----------------------------
 10  11 TRN  TRAIN OPERATING PERSONNEL    25    5  ------XXXXX-----------*****-----------------------
 11  13 PROG  TEST PROGRAM                 0    3  ---------------------------CCC--------------------
 12  13 PUR  PROCURE FORMS                12    8  ------------XXXXXXXX-----------*********-----------
 13  14 OPER PROGRAM OPERATIONAL           0    2  -------------------------------------CC-----------
```

KEY: X EARLY RANGE

       C CRITICAL RANGE

       * LATE RANGE

Figure 7-15. Printed output: bar chart time schedule

still valid; only a relatively small portion of the data deck must be discarded and replaced. The keypunching involved in updating is generally much less than the original keypunching.

The new data deck is run in the same manner as the original data deck was run and the printed output is again analyzed for satisfactory timing. For a complex project, several such computer runs may be necessary to obtain a satisfactory plan and time schedule.

IMPLEMENTATION OF PROJECT

When a satisfactory plan and schedule are derived, the project will be implemented. The early start sort is usually used to get the project "rolling." It will generally be found that soon after work on the project begins, one or more of the assumptions underlying the original plan must be changed. One of the jobs in the project may take longer than was anticipated, one of the jobs may take a shorter time, or a supplier may come in late with the delivery. The assumption that one activity may follow another could also prove to be invalid. Thus, it is important as the project progresses to update both the time estimates and the network logic to indicate any changes in the plan. The process of updating the analysis is portrayed in Figure 7-16.

The effect of a single change or of several minor changes can often be analyzed without an additional computer run. When a large number of changes have taken place in the time estimates or in the diagram itself, it is generally desirable to update the data deck by replacing the activity cards for which the data have changed. The new data deck is then rerun on the computer to produce up-to-date output. For many projects, an updating run is made once every 2 weeks. At certain crucial points in the project, it may be desirable to make updating runs more frequently than every 2 weeks; on a long-term project, updating runs once a month may prove satisfactory.

Computer Output — Bar Chart

These may be used for a substitute of bar charts prepared manually. It may be necessary to arrange the data deck for a special run to have the bar chart to the scheduler's satisfaction. Sorting the cards and getting a computer printout of a bar chart may avoid the necessity of making up the charts manually.

A typical bar chart produced by a computer is shown in Figure 7-15. The "first 40 weeks" are indicated by the horizontal row of

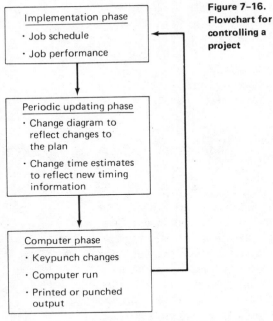

Figure 7–16. Flowchart for controlling a project

Implementation phase

· Job schedule

· Job performance

Periodic updating phase

· Change diagram to reflect changes to the plan

· Change time estimates to reflect new timing information

Computer phase

· Keypunch changes

· Computer run

· Printed or punched output

numbers: 1,2,3,4,5, and so on. As a means of conserving space, week 10 consists of a "0" with a "1" on top of it; week 11, a "1" over a "1"; week 12, a "1" over a "2" and so on.

The "bars" on the graph are made up of these symbols:

X	Early Range
0	Critical Range
*	Late Range

The interpretations of the symbols are indicated by the following information, which applies to the "bars" in Figure 7–15:

- *Job 1,2 — Decide on Computer:* The "bar" for Job 1,2 consists of four 0's, indicating that this 4-week job must be going on during all of these 4 weeks. It is a critical job and there is no leeway in scheduling it. Since it is the first job, it starts at the beginning of the week.
- *Job 2,6 — Procure Computer:*
  Job Time: 25 weeks
  Total Float: 3 weeks
  Early Range: The three X's indicate the "early range." The job can be started any time from the beginning of week 5 to the beginning of week 8. Note that this is the same period of time,

for scheduling purposes, as the end of week 5 (or the end of week 4).

Critical Range: The 22 0's indicate the critical range (22 weeks for Job 2,6) during which the job must be going on. In addition to these 22 weeks on the critical range, 3 weeks can be scheduled within the early and/or late range. This provides flexibility in scheduling and in the use of resources.

Late Range: The three "***" at the end of the "bar" represent the late range. The "early finish" and "late finish" are the ends of the 3-week time period covered by the three asterisks.

If Job 2,6 begins at the earliest start time (the beginning of week 5) . . .	The finish time is indicated by the last 0 (the end of week 29).

----XXX00000000000000000000000***----

If Job 2,6 begins at the latest start time (the beginning of week 8) . . .	The finish time is indicated by the last asterisk (the end of week 32).

SAMPLE BAR FROM COMPUTER BAR GRAPH

- *Job 9,12 — Design Forms:* The "bar" for Job 9,12 is comprised of two X's and two asterisks with 10 hyphens in between. Fourteen weeks are available for the completion of this 2-week job. It can be started from the beginning of the 17th week to the beginning of the 29th week. There is no critical range other than that the job must be started no later than the beginning of the 29th week.

- *Job 13,14 — Program Operational:* The two 0's of the "bar" for Job 13,14 indicate that this 2-week job is on the critical path (has no float) and must start at the beginning of week 39 and finish at the end of week 40.

Calendar Time

In some computer runs, the time span in weeks can be converted to calendar time. It is a matter of personal preference. However, there are some difficulties. For example, the problem of how to handle Sundays and holidays must be resolved through computer programming. Also, the project duration might be reduced because it does not meet management needs. In this situation, it is more efficient not to have the calendar dates in the computer. Once the final date for the project is approved by management, the schedule in weeks can be converted to calendar time.

Reducing the Project Duration

Management may decide that the duration time for a project is too long to meet projected plans. When this happens, it is necessary to analyze the arrow diagram, make adjustments in time estimates, and reschedule the jobs to meet the new deadline. Depending on the scope of the project, a great deal of work may be involved in reducing the duration time. More details will be provided on this subject in succeeding chapters. Briefly, it involves:

1. Analyzing the critical path to determine which jobs can be reduced. For example, the jobs with "0" for total float would be reviewed first. Figure 7–14 lists "total float" for the jobs included in the sample computer installation project. The jobs with "0" in the total float column would be on the critical path and should be analyzed first in determining how to reduce the 40-week duration of the project.

2. Reducing the time required for jobs on the critical path to the extent needed to meet the project deadline. A prime consideration in selecting which jobs should be shortened would be the additional costs incurred.

3. Evaluating what effects reducing the critical path has on other paths in the arrow diagram. If another path has become the critical path, the new critical path must be analyzed and necessary reductions made in the job estimates. This can be done using Figure 7–4. The critical path and next-longest path are as follows:

Critical Path   Job: 1,2 2,3 3,4 4,5 5,6 6,11 11,13 13,14
             Time: $4 + 1 + 5 + 2 + 20 + 3 + 3 + 2 = 40$ weeks

Next-Longest Path   Job: 1,2 2,6 6,11 11,13 13,14
             Time: $4 + 25 + 3 + 3 + 2 = 37$ weeks

If "Prepare Site" (5,6) is reduced 3 weeks, there will be two critical paths; if 4 weeks or more is taken out of this path, the next-longest path will then become the critical path. If further reductions are made in these two paths, a point will be reached where another path on the network will also become a critical path.

Accuracy of the Scheduling

It should be emphasized that the scheduling process in the project management cycle is highly dependent on time estimates. If there is a weakness in any scheduling system, it is in time estimating. If people provide inaccurate time estimates, the total time will be inaccurate.

There is an orderly procedure to follow in analyzing these estimates. Briefly, this consists of examining jobs on the critical path first, then jobs on the next-longest path, and so on — questioning and revising time estimates that seem out of line until a satisfactory project schedule is developed.

SUMMARY

There are many benefits to be derived from using the computer with the network planning method. With the computer, it is possible:

1. To apply the network planning method very rapidly to large projects that would require many hours of manual calculation.

2. To handle accurately a complex project in which manual calculations would inevitably be subject to errors.

3. To make updating runs as often as desired without excessive expenditure of time.

4. To print in useful and readable format the results of the computer analysis.

5. To undertake time/cost trade-off analysis and resource-leveling analysis that would be difficult and extremely time consuming to do manually.

8

PERT / Time

PERT (Project Evaluation Review Technique) is a technique that can be used to plan, schedule, and control activities that must be completed to finish a project. Developed in the late 1950s for the Special Projects Office of the Navy Bureau of Ordnance, PERT was used initially to plan and coordinate the work of some 3,000 contractors and agencies for the Polaris missile program. The use of PERT is credited with advancing successful completion of the Polaris program more than 2 years.

PERT and CPM are similar in concept: both use arrow diagrams, calculate critical paths and floats, and use computers to carry out detailed calculations. The two techniques differ in several significant details:

1. PERT is "event-oriented."

2. PERT uses three time estimates for each activity.

3. PERT calculates the probability of meeting a scheduled date.

Definition of Terms

PROJECT: A project is defined as a network of activities and

The material in Chapter 8 is taken from *Philco Manual TM-19 PERT Systems*, April 1962, and *TM-30 PERT III Systems*.

events having well-defined starting and ending points.

EVENT: An event is the starting and/or ending point of an activity. Events designate either specific accomplishments or points at which programs start.

ACTIVITY: An activity is a time-consuming element of a project which is defined by a predecessor and successor event. An activity cannot start until its predecessor event is completed.

SLACK FLOAT: The slack float of an event is the time interval until the completion date of the end event.

ESTABLISHING THE NETWORK

After setting objectives, the first step in planning a PERT system is to determine the activities that must be accomplished. When qualified individuals have determined what activities are required, an arrow diagram is developed that accurately depicts the interrelations—which activity must come first, second, and so on, and which activities can be performed concurrently with others.

Each activity in the project is represented by an arrow and label on the diagram. It should be noted, however, that, in contrast with CPM networks, in which activities are labeled, in the PERT network the nodes or events are labeled. For example, Event 1 in a network might have the title "Contract Awarded"; Event 2, "Start Computer Design"; and so on.

OBTAINING TIME ESTIMATES

Time estimates are obtained from a person who is very familiar with the project. The three time estimates—optimistic, most likely, and pessimistic—for each activity are used to offset the bias that is usually present in one time estimate. The range of the time estimates also gives some indication of the scheduling risk involved; for example, a wide spread between the estimates shows considerable uncertainty about the time actually required to accomplish an activity.

Generally, PERT programs require that time estimates be converted into calendar dates, because military users have found this method convenient for their purposes. The computer program usually translates calendar days into weeks and fractions of weeks.

Calendar scheduled dates, or contractual dates, may also be recorded in the PERT diagram. These scheduled dates tend to complicate the job of obtaining realistic time estimates, in that persons tend to give estimates that fit into the time available. This effect may be minimized by securing time estimates for various activities independently, by aggregating estimates for small sections of the network separately, and by releasing scheduled dates only after the detailed time estimates have been obtained. The dates derived by looking at the work content can then be compared to the schedule to see whether discrepancies exist.

Most Likely Time (or Normal Time)

The first time estimate requested is the most likely time. It is the time that would be most frequently required if the activity were repeated many times under similar conditions. It is also the job time estimate that would be used in the critical path method. In a frequency distribution, the most likely time would be the *mode* of the distribution. On the histogram (Figure 8-1), the time period 5 has the greatest frequency (6).

Optimistic Time

The shortest possible time required for completing an activity is the optimistic time. Here it is assumed that everything goes as planned: deliveries of material occur on schedule, machines operate without major breakdowns, personnel perform work within work standards, and the like. The time period 3 on the frequency distribution (Figure 8-1) would represent the optimistic time.

Pessimistic Time

The maximum possible time required to complete an activity is termed the pessimistic time. This is the time required for doing some-

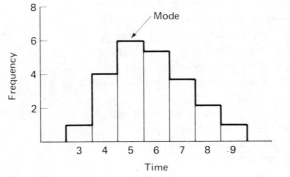

Figure 8-1.
Frequency distribution chart

thing if everything goes wrong simultaneously—in short, the worst possible situation. On the histogram (Figure 8-1) the pessimistic time is 9.

SAMPLE PERT NETWORK

The three time estimates obtained for each activity in the project can be recorded on the PERT network to aid in the planning stage. For illustration purposes, a sample PERT network is shown in Figure 8-2 with the time estimates indicated. There are six events (figures in circles) in the network: 1, 2, 3, 4, 5, and 6. The events are connected by arrows representing eight activities or jobs to which the sets of three time estimates have been recorded:

Activity	Time Estimates (Weeks)
1,2	1–3–8
2,3	3–6–9
2,4	1–2–3
etc.	

Figure 8-2. PERT network time estimates

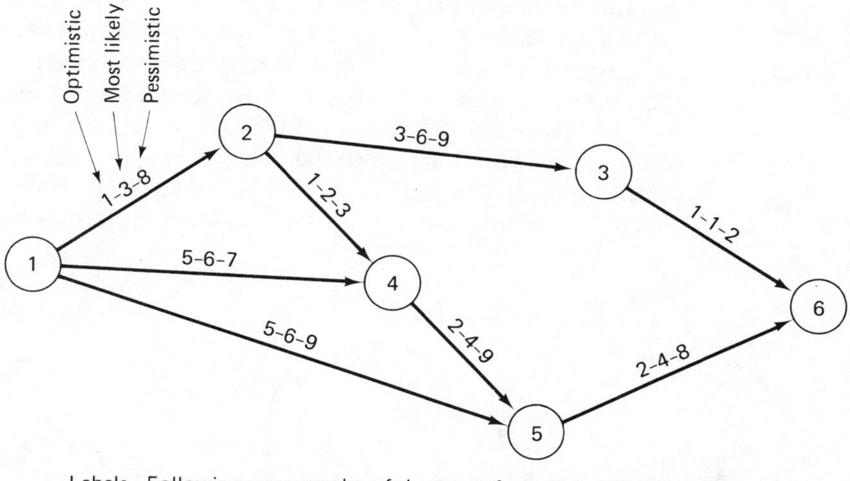

Labels. Following are examples of the type of word identifications that are listed on a PERT diagram inside each node and on each activity arrow:

Node	Designation	Activity	Designation
1	Start design	1, 2	Electrical design
2	Finish electrical design	2, 3	Order components
3	Component delivery	3, 6	Test components
Etc.		Etc.	

This sample network with six events and eight activities will be used to explain the principles involved in making PERT timing calculations. For a network with, say, more than 100 activities, a computer is used to perform the timing calculations.

CALCULATING THE EXPECTED (MEAN) TIME AND VARIANCE

With the three time estimates, the expected (mean) time (t_e) and variance $(\sigma_{t_e})^2$ of an activity performance time can be derived. Statisticians have provided formulas for calculating t_e and $(\sigma_{t_e})^2$ for an activity.

Distribution of Time Estimates

The basic factors used in the formulas — the three time estimates — can be translated into a distribution curve, which may resemble one of the curves shown in Figure 8-3.

The location of the time estimates on the time scale determines the type of curve that might represent the distribution — the spread of a (optimistic time) and b (pessimistic time) and the location of m (most likely time) within the spread. To illustrate, the histogram in Figure 8-4(a) (with a distribution curve added) depicts the frequency of occurrences for different time intervals at which an activity might be completed if it were performed many times.

In Figure 8-4(b) the three time estimates represented by the histogram are located on the distribution curve. It is assumed that the curve has only one peak — the most likely time for completion. The m on this peak represents the completion date that has the

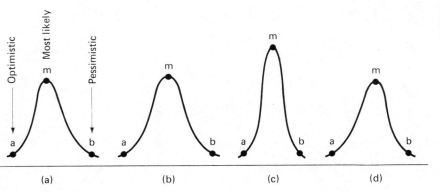

Figure 8-3.
Sample distribution curves

(a)   (b)   (c)   (d)

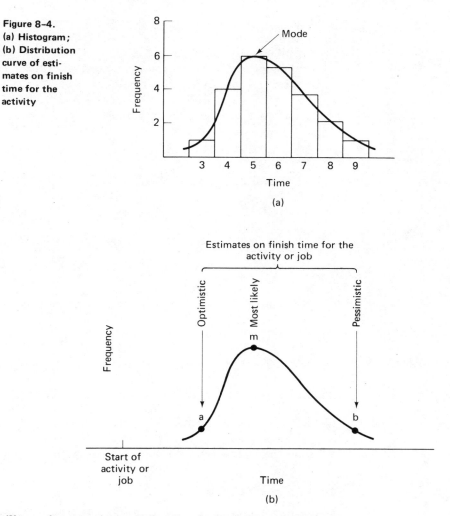

Figure 8-4.
(a) Histogram;
(b) Distribution
curve of esti-
mates on finish
time for the
activity

greatest probability of occurring, while the low points, *a* and *b*, indicate dates that have a small chance of being realized.

Formula for Expected (Mean) Time

The three time estimates for each activity are used in calculating a single weighted average or mean called the *expected time* (t_e) of the activity. The expected time is derived from the optimistic, most likely, and pessimistic times by this formula:

$$t_e = \frac{a + 4m + b}{6}$$

The symbols a, m, and b represent the three time estimates: a for the optimistic; b, the most likely (or normal); and c, the pessimistic. The result of the formula is a weighted average with two-thirds of the weight given to the most likely (normal) time; one-sixth, to the optimistic; and one-sixth, to the pessimistic.

Example: The expected times for the activities on the sample PERT network are derived from the specified sets of time estimates (Figure 8-2) by applying the formula for t_e.

Activity	*Time Estimates* Opti-mistic (a)	Most Likely (m)	Pessi-mistic (b)	The Calculation	Expected Time, t_e (Weeks)
1,2	1	3	8	$\dfrac{1 + 4(3) + 8}{6}$ =	3.5
1,5	5	6	9	$\dfrac{5 + 4(6) + 9}{6}$ =	6.3
2,3	3	6	9	$\dfrac{3 + 4(6) + 9}{6}$ =	6.0
etc.					

All of the expected times are recorded on the network shown in Figure 8-5. Figure 8-6 indicates the location of t_e, the expected time, on the four distribution curves shown previously in Figure 8-3.

Formula for Variance

In the PERT system, *variance* is a term that describes the uncertainty associated with how much time will be required to accomplish an activity or the entire project. If the variance is large (which indicates that the optimistic and pessimistic estimates are far apart), there is great uncertainty as to when the activity will be completed. On the other hand, a small variance indicates very little uncertainty. By inspection one can guess that the expected time for Figure 8-6(a) will have a larger variance than the expected time for 8-6(c). In statistical terms, the variance is equal to the standard deviation squared:

$$\text{Variance} = (\sigma_{t_e})^2$$

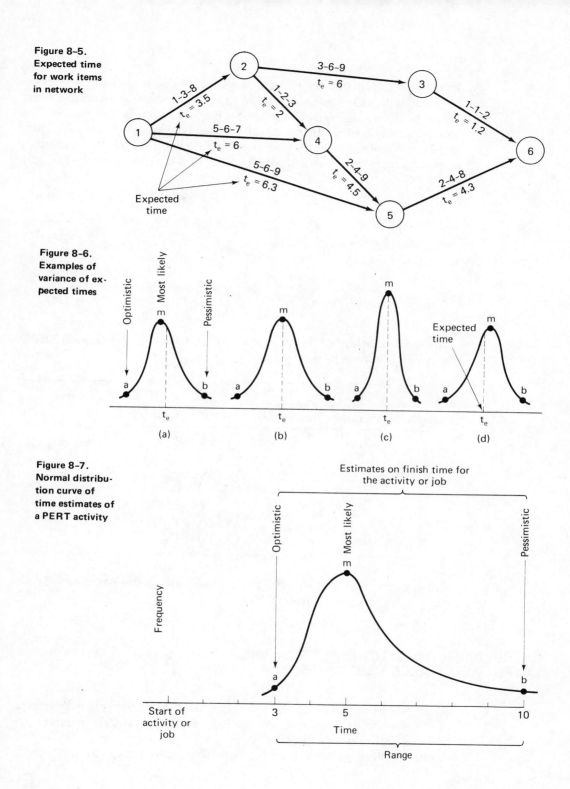

**Figure 8-5.
Expected time
for work items
in network**

Expected
time

**Figure 8-6.
Examples of
variance of ex-
pected times**

Optimistic   Most likely   Pessimistic

m

a   b

t_e

(a)

m

a   b

t_e

(b)

m

a   b

t_e

(c)

Expected
time

m

a   b

t_e

(d)

**Figure 8-7.
Normal distribu-
tion curve of
time estimates of
a PERT activity**

Estimates on finish time for
the activity or job

Optimistic   Most likely   Pessimistic

m

Frequency

a   b

Start of
activity or
job

3   5   10

Time

Range

The *standard deviation* (σ) is a measure of the spread of a distribution. It is the root mean square of the deviations of the various items from their average. For the purposes here, the standard deviation can be approximated as being equal to one-sixth of the range. To illustrate the calculation of the standard deviation and the variance, consider an activity with time estimates of 3–5–10 (Figure 8–7).

	The Formula	*The Calculation*
The range is	$b - a$	$10 - 3 = 7$
The standard deviation (σ) is approximately	$\dfrac{b - a}{6}$	$\dfrac{10 - 3}{6} = \dfrac{7}{6} = 1.17$
The variance $(\sigma_{t_e})^2$ is	$\left(\dfrac{b - a}{6}\right)^2$	$(1.17)^2 = 1.37$

The computation of variance for the activities in the sample PERT network is shown in the following:

Activity	Time Optimistic	Time Pessimistic	The Calculation	Variance $(\sigma_{t_e})^2$
1,2	1	8	$\left(\dfrac{8-1}{6}\right)^2 = \left(\dfrac{7}{6}\right)^2 = (1.17)^2 =$	1.37
1,4	5	7	$\left(\dfrac{7-5}{6}\right)^2 = \left(\dfrac{2}{6}\right)^2 = \dfrac{1}{9} =$	0.11
1,5	5	9	$\left(\dfrac{9-5}{6}\right)^2 = \left(\dfrac{4}{6}\right)^2 = \dfrac{4}{9} =$	0.44

The sample PERT network, Figure 8–8, shows the variances for all eight activities in the project.

CALCULATING EARLIEST EXPECTED TIME, LATEST ALLOWABLE TIME, AND SLACK

With the PERT system, the interest is primarily in events — the starts and finishes of activities. An activity represents work, whereas an event signifies a point in time.

The earliest expected and latest allowable times for an event,

**Figure 8-8.
Time variances
for PERT
activities**

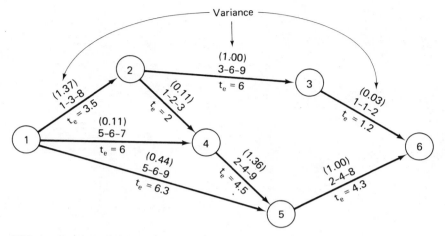

and slack (the difference between the two), are a part of the basic data required in scheduling and controlling a PERT project.

Earliest Expected Time

For each event in the network, an *earliest expected time of completion* (T_E) is computed. The T_E for an event is the total obtained by adding the t_e's (expected times) for the activities on the longest path (in terms of time) that leads to the event. The computation of earliest expected times begins with the first event and continues with the second, and so on, to the end of the project.

The Formula: The first event is established as time zero. For all other events, the computation for determining T_E consists of the following:

$$T_E \text{ for Event } X =$$

$$\left(\begin{array}{l} T_E \text{ for event immediately} \\ \text{preceding Event } X \end{array} \right) - \left(\begin{array}{l} t_e \text{ for activity immediately} \\ \text{preceding Event } X \end{array} \right)$$

If more than one path leads into Event X, perform the computations for all such paths and use the *largest* total as the T_E for Event X.

Example: The PERT network for the sample project (Figure 8-9) is used to illustrate the calculation of T_E.

		Earliest Expected Time, T_E
Event 1	The earliest expected time for the first event in the project is established as Time 0.	0

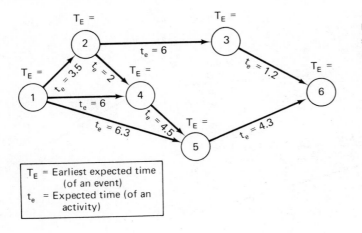

Figure 8-9.
PERT network
showing expect-
ing times

T_E = Earliest expected time
(of an event)
t_e = Expected time (of an
activity)

Event 2   The longest path — and the only one —
leading to Event 2 consists of Activity 1,2.
This activity has an expected time of 3.5
weeks.

$$\frac{T_E \text{ for Event 1}}{0} + \frac{t_e \text{ for Activity 1,2}}{3.5} = 3.5 \qquad 3.5$$

Event 3   The only path leading to Event 3 is via
Activity 2,3. To the T_E for Event 2,
add the t_e for Activity 2,3:

$$3.5 + 6 = 9.5 \qquad 9.5$$

(See Figure 8-10.)

Event 4   Two paths lead to Event 4 — (a) via Activity
2,3; and (b) via Activity 1,4:

(a) $\dfrac{T_E \text{ for Event 2}}{3.5} + \dfrac{t_e \text{ for Activity 2,4}}{2} = 5.5$

(b) $\dfrac{T_E \text{ for Event 1}}{0} + \dfrac{t_e \text{ for Activity 1,4}}{6} = 6$

Use the *largest* time factor. (See Figure
8-11.) 6

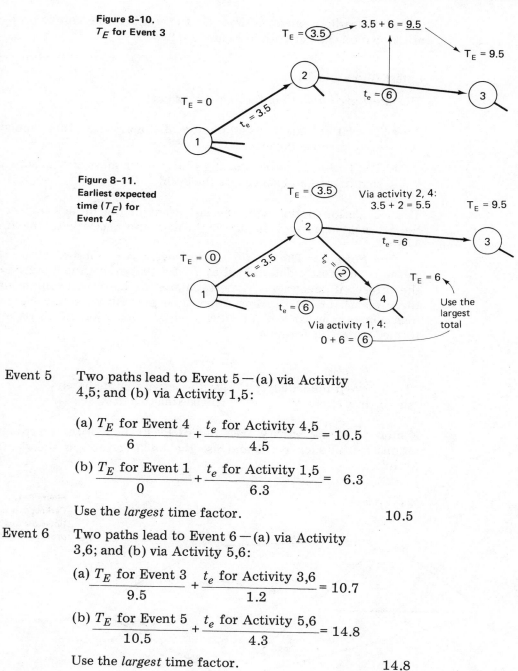

Figure 8-10.
T_E for Event 3

Figure 8-11.
Earliest expected time (T_E) for Event 4

Event 5   Two paths lead to Event 5 — (a) via Activity 4,5; and (b) via Activity 1,5:

(a) $\dfrac{T_E \text{ for Event 4}}{6} + \dfrac{t_e \text{ for Activity 4,5}}{4.5} = 10.5$

(b) $\dfrac{T_E \text{ for Event 1}}{0} + \dfrac{t_e \text{ for Activity 1,5}}{6.3} = 6.3$

Use the *largest* time factor.   10.5

Event 6   Two paths lead to Event 6 — (a) via Activity 3,6; and (b) via Activity 5,6:

(a) $\dfrac{T_E \text{ for Event 3}}{9.5} + \dfrac{t_e \text{ for Activity 3,6}}{1.2} = 10.7$

(b) $\dfrac{T_E \text{ for Event 5}}{10.5} + \dfrac{t_e \text{ for Activity 5,6}}{4.3} = 14.8$

Use the *largest* time factor.   14.8

All of the earliest expected times for the events in the sample project are shown on the network in Figure 8-12.

Latest Allowable Time

The *latest allowable time* for an event is both:

- The latest time for completion of the activities that immediately precede the event.
- The latest allowable starting time for the most critical activity that immediately succeeds the event.

The calculation begins with the last event in the project and continues back in reverse sequence through the network to the first event.

The Formula: The T_L for the last event is established either (1) as the time already determined as T_E for that event (the duration of the project if the original time estimates are used in accomplishing the project), or (2) as some other time prescribed on the basis of management needs. For all other events, calculation of T_L is performed using this formula:

$$T_L \text{ for Event } X =$$

$$\left(\begin{array}{l} T_L \text{ for event immediately} \\ \text{succeeding Event } X \end{array} \right) - \left(\begin{array}{l} t_e \text{ for activity immediately} \\ \text{succeeding Event } X \end{array} \right)$$

If more than one activity leads out of Event X, perform the computations for all such paths and use the *smallest* total as the T_L for Event X.

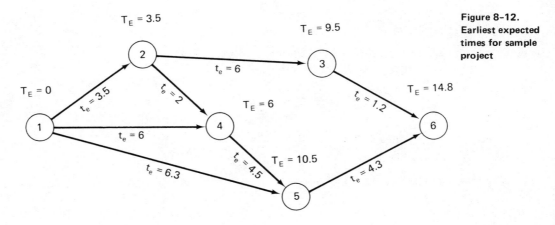

Figure 8-12.
Earliest expected times for sample project

Example (using the sample project network):

		Latest Allowable Time, T_L
Event 6	The latest allowable time for the last event in the project is established as 14.8, which is the T_E for Event 6 and also the project duration.	14.8
Event 5	One path leads out of Event 5 — Activity 5,6. The calculation:	

$$\underset{14.8}{\underline{T_L \text{ for Event 6}}} - \underset{4.3}{\underline{t_e \text{ for Activity 5,6}}} = \qquad 10.5$$

(See Figure 8–13.)

Event 4	One path leads out of Event 4 — Activity 4,5, which has a t_e of 4.5 weeks.	

$$10.5 - 4.5 = \qquad 6.0$$

Event 3	One path leads out of Event 3 — Activity 3,6, with a t_e of 1.2 weeks.	

$$14.8 - 1.2 = \qquad 13.6$$

Event 2	Two paths lead out of Event 2 — (a) via Activity 2,3; and (b) via Activity 2,4:	

$$\text{(a) } \underset{13.6}{\underline{T_L \text{ for Event 3}}} - \underset{6}{\underline{t_e \text{ for Activity 2,3}}} = \qquad 7.6$$

$$\text{(b) } \underset{6}{\underline{T_L \text{ for Event 4}}} - \underset{2}{\underline{t_e \text{ for Activity 2,4}}} = \qquad 4.0$$

Use the *smallest* time factor. (See Figure 8–14.)   4.0

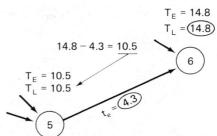

Figure 8–13.
Latest allowable
time (T_L) for
Event 5

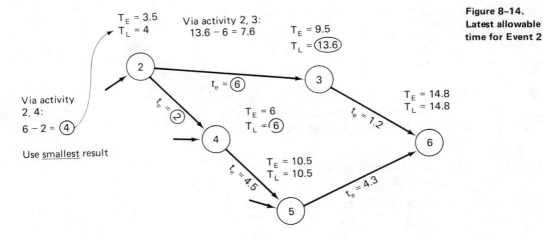

Figure 8-14.
Latest allowable
time for Event 2

Event 1   Three paths lead out of Event 1, via these
activities: (a) 1,2; (b) 1,4; and (c) 1,5.

(a) 4 − 3.5 = 0.5
(b) 6 − 6 = 0
(c) 10.5 − 6.3 = 4.2

Use the *smallest* time factor.   0

The network for the sample project, shown in Figure 8-15, includes
all of the latest allowable times for events.

Slack (Event)

The *slack* of an event is the amount of time that the "completion of
the event" can be delayed (if any) without advancing the completion date of the project. This "event-oriented" terminology means
that, for example, if an event has 4 weeks slack, there is a 4-week
interval between the two times given below:

1. The earliest time all activities immediately preceding the
   event will be completed according to the original time estimates (the earliest expected time, T_E).

2. The latest starting time for the most critical activity that
   succeeds the event (the latest allowable time, T_L).

The slack data are of great value in scheduling and controlling a
project.

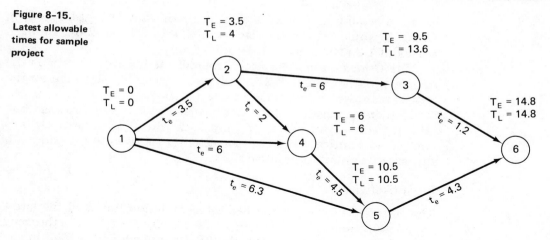

Figure 8–15.
Latest allowable
times for sample
project

The formula for calculating slack is:

$$T_L - T_E$$

Example: Following are the calculations of slack for the events in the sample project:

Event	$T_L{}^*$	–	$T_E{}^*$	=	Slack (Event)
1	0	–	0	=	0
2	4	–	3.5	=	0.5
3	13.6	–	9.5	=	4.1
4	6	–	6	=	0
5	10.5	–	10.5	=	0
6	14.8	–	14.8	=	0

*See Figure 8–16.

This PERT example includes events with zero slack and with positive slack (T_L is greater than T_E). In the PERT system, slack can also be negative (T_L is less than T_E). This negative slack occurs when the project duration according to the original time estimates is longer than that required to meet management needs.

To illustrate, assume the project in the sample PERT network (Figure 8–15) must be completed in 12 rather than in 14.8 weeks. All of the T_L figures in the network would have to be recomputed on the basis of the 12-week project duration:

> For Event 6, the T_L would be 12
> For Event 5, 7.7
> etc.

Event 6 would then have a slack time of –2.8 (12 – 14.8 = –2.8); Event 5 would have –2.8 slack time (7.7 – 10.5 = –2.8); Event 3 a slack of 1.3 (10.8 – 9.5 = 1.3); and so on.

The Critical Path: The slack data indicate the critical path on the sample project (Figure 8-16.) All events with "0" slack are on the critical path, which follows the route 1–4–5–6.

If there is negative slack, the project may have more than one critical path. In this situation, any path with 0 or negative slack is considered a critical path. Greatest attention is given to the path with the largest amount of negative slack.

Float (Activity)

The difference between the earliest completion time and the latest completion time for an activity is the *activity float.* This is the same "float" that was calculated in the CPM approach and is used in the same manner.

The formula for calculating activity slack for Activity X is:

$$\begin{pmatrix} \text{Latest completion} \\ \text{time for Activity } X, \\ \text{or } T_L \text{ for the end} \\ \text{event of Activity } X \end{pmatrix} - \begin{pmatrix} \text{Earliest start} \\ \text{time for Activity} \\ X, \text{ or } T_E \text{ for the} \\ \text{beginning event of} \\ \text{Activity } X \end{pmatrix}$$

$$- \begin{pmatrix} \text{Duration} \\ \text{of} \\ \text{Activity } X, \\ \text{or } t_e \end{pmatrix} = \text{Float}$$

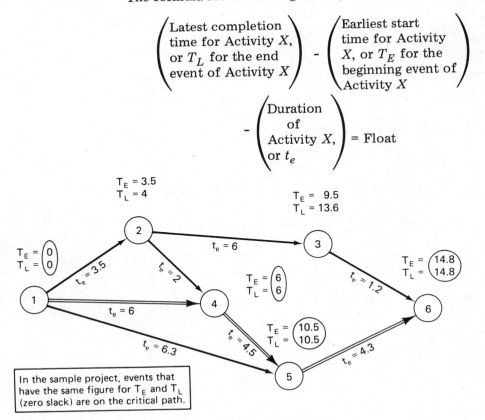

Figure 8-16. Sample network showing critical path

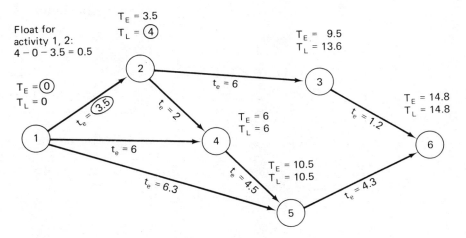

Figure 8-17. Sample PERT network

Example (using the sample PERT network):

Activity	T_L, Event 2	T_E, Event 1	t_e	Float
1,2	4	– 0	– 3.5 =	0.5

(See Figure 8–17.)

$$1,4 \qquad \frac{T_L, \text{ Event 4}}{6} - \frac{T_E, \text{ Event 1}}{0} - \frac{t_e}{6} = 0$$

$$1,5 \qquad \frac{T_L, \text{ Event 5}}{10.5} - \frac{T_E, \text{ Event 1}}{0} - \frac{t_e}{6.3} = 4.2$$

$$2,4 \qquad \frac{T_L, \text{ Event 4}}{6} - \frac{T_E, \text{ Event 2}}{3.5} - \frac{t_e}{2} = 0.5$$

etc.

CALCULATING PROBABILITY

One of the features of PERT is that it provides a method of estimating the *probability* that a schedule date can be met. Statisticians have provided the following formula for making this estimate:

$$Z = \frac{T_S - T_E}{\sigma T_E}$$

where Z = measure related to the probability of meeting the scheduled date

T_S = scheduled time for the event

T_E = expected time for the event

σ_{T_E} = standard deviation — the square root of the sum of the variances of the activities used in calculating the T_E for the event

Example: A scheduled time of 13 weeks has been set for completion of the sample project. The expected time for completing the project is 14.8 weeks. Determine the probability of meeting the scheduled date.

$$T_S = 13$$

$$T_E = 14.3$$

σ_{T_E} = square root of variances for activities used in calculating T_E for Event 6 (see Figure 8–18):

Activity	Variance
1,4	0.11
4,5	1.36
5,6	1.00
	2.47

$$\sqrt{2.47} = 1.57$$

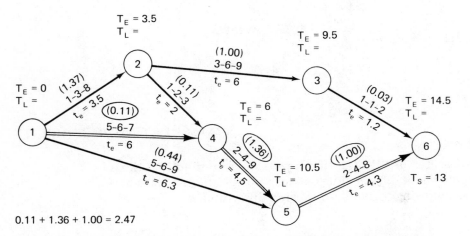

0.11 + 1.36 + 1.00 = 2.47

Figure 8–18. Sum of the variances of activities used in calculating T_E for Event 6

Figure 8–19.
Table of values
of areas under
the normal
curve

Z	O	Z	O
0.0	0.5000	−3.0	0.0013
0.1	0.5398	−2.9	0.0019
0.2	0.5793	−2.8	0.0026
0.3	0.6179	−2.7	0.0035
0.4	0.6554	−2.6	0.0047
0.5	0.6915	−2.5	0.0062
0.6	0.7257	−2.4	0.0082
0.7	0.7580	−2.3	0.0107
0.8	0.7881	−2.2	0.0139
0.9	0.8159	−2.1	0.0179
1.0	0.8413	−2.0	0.0228
1.1	0.8643	−1.9	0.0287
1.2	0.8849	−1.8	0.0359
1.3	0.9032	−1.7	0.0446
1.4	0.9192	−1.6	0.0548
1.5	0.9332	−1.5	0.0668
1.6	0.9452	−1.4	0.0808
1.7	0.9554	−1.3	0.0968
1.8	0.9641	−1.2	0.1151
1.9	0.9713	−1.1	0.1357
2.0	0.9772	−1.0	0.1587
2.1	0.9821	−0.9	0.1841
2.2	0.9861	−0.8	0.2119
2.3	0.9893	−0.7	0.2420
2.4	0.9918	−0.6	0.2743
2.5	0.9938	−0.5	0.3085
2.6	0.9953	−0.4	0.3446
2.7	0.9965	−0.3	0.3821
2.8	0.9974	−0.2	0.4207
2.9	0.9981	−0.1	0.4602
		−0.0	0.5000
3.0	0.9987		

A standard table found in most mathematics and statistical handbooks.

These values are substituted in the formula

$$Z = \frac{T_S - T_E}{\sigma T_E}$$

$$Z = \frac{13 - 14.8}{\sqrt{2.47}} = \frac{-1.8}{1.57} = -1.1$$

Using the table of values of areas under the normal curve shown in Figure 8–19, for a Z of −1.1, the probability is 0.1357. This means that there is a 13.57% chance of meeting the scheduled date of 13 weeks for the project.

SUMMARY

The three time estimates in PERT — optimistic, most likely, and pessimistic — provide a basis for calculating the expected (mean) time (t_e) and variance $(\sigma_{t_e})^2$ for each activity in the project. The expected time for an activity is used in the project schedule; the variance is used in evaluating the scheduling risk involved in the expected time.

The expected times for activities are then used in calculating the earliest expected time (T_E) and the latest allowable time (T_L). With these data, the slack for each event and the float for each activity are computed.

Finally, the probability of meeting the planned target date is determined.

The PERT system of planning, scheduling, and controlling a project is considered by many practitioners to be superior to the critical path method for research and development projects where many uncertainties about the schedule exist. The use of the three time estimates brings these uncertainties clearly into focus. The probability of completing the project on time is also a useful number to those versed in probability theory.

In recent practice, however, many PERT users have dropped the probability features. Several problems have been encountered with them. One is that estimators tend to be overly pessimistic when giving pessimistic times, thereby biasing project completing time toward the pessimistic side. Another is that the validity of the probability calculations themselves has been questioned.

Some installations are now using "activity-oriented" rather than "event-oriented" PERT. In the case where probabilities have been dropped and activity-oriented PERT is used, one has difficulty in seeing any differences between PERT and CPM.

Since the development of the PERT/COST system, which is discussed in Chapter 9, it is customary to refer to the PERT concept described above as PERT/TIME.

The similarities between PERT and CPM are very pronounced and it appears that the PERT originators had knowledge of CPM before they derived their system. It is interesting to note, however, that to date the author is not aware of any extension to PERT that considers the time/cost compression aspect, which is such a valuable extension of CPM.

PERT/COST

There is a continuing need for management methods that will assist in defining the work to be performed and in developing more realistic schedule and cost estimates based on the resources planned to perform the work. These methods should also assist in determining where resources should be applied to best achieve the time, cost, and technical performance objectives; and in identifying those areas developing potential delays or cost overruns in time to permit corrective action. For example, managers at each level should be able to determine:

1. Whether the current estimated time and cost for completing the entire project are realistic.

2. Whether the project is meeting the committed schedule and cost estimate and, if not, the extent of any difference.

The first step is to prepare a feasible PERT plan and schedule. Next, the PERT/COST technique requires periodic comparisons of the actual costs incurred for each activity and the actual time ob-

The material in Chapter 9 is presented in a condensed and modified form from the *DOD and NASA Guide, PERT/COST Systems Design*, Office of the Secretary of Defense and National Aeronautics and Space Administration.

served by each activity with their original estimates. This comparison significantly improves cost and schedule control by establishing the cost and time status of the project and identifying any potential cost overruns and schedule slippages. Estimates of cost and time needed to complete work not yet started are also obtained in order to predict future slippages and cost overruns.

PERT/COST REPORTS

The basic information generated in the PERT/COST system can be summarized in several ways for program management reporting. The format and detail depend upon the planning and control requirements of each level of management and vary accordingly. Essentially, the reports provide the following information:

- The current project plan, schedule, and budget
- Time and cost performance to date, in relation to the plan
- Time and cost projections for completion of the project objectives

These PERT/COST reports point out potential trouble spots in the project and make it possible for managers to anticipate schedule slippages and cost overruns/underruns. Since the reports rank problem areas according to how critically these areas affect the total project, managers know where their attention is most urgently needed.

The PERT/COST reports summarize current information without distortion to each level of project management, thereby relieving a manager of the need to review detailed data from subordinate levels in order to evaluate project status. However, this detailed information is available without additional processing should any specific area require analysis.

All the PERT/COST reports are interrelated, each dealing with the same basic data, but each emphasizing a different element of the project.

PERT/COST reports would usually be prepared on a monthly basis to coincide with normal accounting procedures. However, reporting can be done more frequently if required or desired.

Management Summary Report

The PERT/COST *management summary report* (Figure 9-1) shows the overall schedule and cost status of the project as a whole as well

PERT/COST Management summary report

Program: MWS | Summary level: 4 - Controls | Report covers the period: 1 July 1961 – 31 March 1962
Project: A10 Vehicle | Contractor: | Date this

Summary level: 4 - Case | Report covers the period: 1 July 1961 – 31 March 1962

Summary level: 3 - Propulsion | Report covers the period: 1 July 1961 – 31 March 1962
Contractor: Missile Systems Co. | Contract number 659 | Date this report: 3/31/62

Item	Cost of work — Work performed to date $			Totals at completion $			Schedule	Day	Slack status (weeks)	Remarks
	Original estimate	Actual costs	Overrun (underrun)	Contract estimate	Latest revised estimate	Projected overrun (underrun)	1961 / 1962 / 1963			
Total propulsion	850,000	1,050,000	200,000	2,500,000	2,850,000	350,000	L E *	28 / 31	–8.0	1. Case (S, O) 2. Controls (O)
Case	72,000	186,000	114,000	596,000	814,000	218,000	L E *	12 / 17	–8.0	1. Mounting (S, O)
Controls	392,000	411,000	19,000	704,000	793,000	89,000	E L *	27 / 05	10.0	1. Staging transducer (O)
Servo	126,000	174,000	48,000	387,000	447,000	60,000	E L *	18 / 02	2.0	
Nozzles	67,000	64,000	(3,000)	378,000	346,000	(32,000)	L E *	28 / 31	–8.0	1. Cone (S, U)
Ignition	114,000	141,000	27,000	262,000	279,000	17,000	E L *	08 / 12	5.0	
Auxiliary power units	79,000	74,000	(5,000)	173,000	171,000	(2,000)	E L *	31 / 31	4.0	

Schedule legend:
* – Scheduled completion date of total item
E – Earliest completion date } Of most critical element within item
L – Latest completion date

1961: J A S O N D 1962: J F M A M J J A S O N D 1963: J F M A M J

Time now

Remarks legend:
S = Schedule slippage
O = Cost overrun
U = Cost underrun

Figure 9–1. PERT/COST management summary report

as each of the major component items. The report provides the following information:

- *The cost overrun/underrun to date*, through a comparison of the estimated costs with actual costs for the work performed.
- *The projection of cost overrun/underrun for the total project*, which is obtained by comparing the original cost estimate for the project with actual costs plus the estimated costs to complete the project.
- *The amount of schedule slippage*, as indicated by the difference between the established schedule for project completion and the present expected date for project completion.
- *The identification of trouble spots* — identification of those areas of the project where cost or time status requires management attention.

In the example, the manager responsible for the propulsion effort would see that:

- The Propulsion System Development Effort, scheduled for completion on January 31, 1963, is now expected to be completed on March 28, a slippage of 8 weeks.
- There is a cost overrun to date of $200,000 and a projected $350,000 overrun at project completion.
- The case is the major contributor to this cost overrun, and it is also critical in terms of completing the project on schedule.
- The nozzles, also critical to the total effort, show both a cost underrun and a time slippage, and may require more resources to get back on schedule.
- The controls effort is ahead of schedule but shows a cost overrun which might indicate that extra costs are being incurred unnecessarily.

In analyzing the status of a project, the responsible manager would examine the reports for those items where trouble is indicated. He or she would then refer to the lower-level reports as required to isolate the trouble.

Labor Loading Reports and Displays

These reports are used by management to plan the application of personnel and determine the need for overtime, additional hiring, or rescheduling of activities. The *labor loading display* (Figure 9–2)

Figure 9–2. Labor loading display

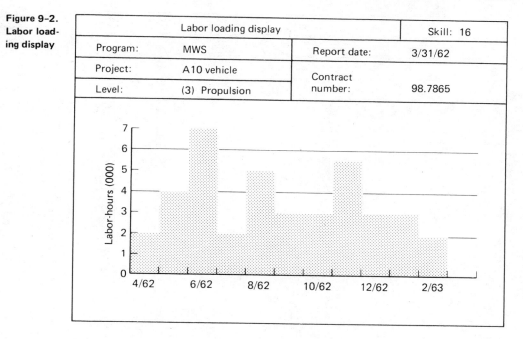

Labor loading display			Skill: 16
Program:	MWS	Report date:	3/31/62
Project:	A10 vehicle	Contract number:	98.7865
Level:	(3) Propulsion		

shows the overall requirements for drafting labor, while the *labor loading report* (Figure 9–3) indicates the allocation of labor-hours among the various jobs.

Referring to the labor loading display and report examples, the manager can determine that:

- The irregular loading pattern may make overtime necessary in some months, even though preceding or succeeding months have unused capacity.

- The heavy loading in June 1962 is tentatively planned largely for a job with positive slack (Charge Number 39784213), while in the same time period there is a job with negative slack (39786340) which might benefit from those resources.

- The heavy loading in June 1962 could be reduced by shifting resources within some activities from June to July or by rescheduling slack activities for July, thereby lowering the labor requirement in June.

Cost-of-Work Report

The *cost-of-work report* shows:

1. The budgeted costs to perform the work.

Labor loading report			Skill: 16	
Program:	MWS	Report date:		3/31/62
Project:	A10 Vehicle	Contract number:		98.7865
Level:	(3) Propulsion			
Month	Performing unit	Charge no.	Estimated labor-hours	Activity slack (weeks)
6/62	6821	39786340	1000	−4.0
	6821	39782191	2000	8.0
	5211	39784213	4000	12.0
			7000*	
7/62	6821	39782315	800	1.0
	6821	39782191	1000	8.0
	5211	39784213	200	12.0
			2000*	

Figure 9–3.
Labor loading report

2. The actual costs to date.

3. The contract estimate for the work performed to date.

4. The projection of costs to project completion, based on actual costs to date and estimates-to-complete for work not yet performed.

The first two points are obtained from the financial plan. The third point is the sum of the latest revised estimates appearing on the project status report. The final point measures the progress achieved in the project. By comparing the actual costs accumulated and the contract estimate for the work performed, the manager can find out if the work is performed at a cost that is greater or less than planned.

The contract estimate for the work performed is used to identify the committed cost estimate planned for the progress achieved to date. It can be represented in this way:

$$\text{Contract estimate for all work performed to date} = \Sigma \left(\frac{A}{R} \times C \right)$$

where A = actual cost to date for a completed or in-progress work package

R = latest revised estimate for a completed or in-progress work package

C = contract cost estimate for a completed or in-progress work package

Since the project has been subdivided into work packages that must be accomplished, the PERT/COST system attempts to relate cost to progress achieved to date by comparing actual costs with the equivalent estimated costs for each work package, and then summing the resultant overruns or underruns to determine the overall status of the project.

In the example (Figure 9–4), the manager can quickly determine that:

- The project is $135,000 under budget in terms of the time-phased cost plan to March 1962.
- The project is $200,000 over the cost estimate for the work completed.
- A $350,000 overrun is anticipated at the project completion.
- A schedule slippage of 8 weeks is predicted for the project.

Schedule and Cost Outlook Reports

The *cost outlook report* (Figure 9–5) and the *schedule outlook report* (Figure 9–6) show the trend of successive monthly projections of the time and cost to complete the work. Each month, new projections are obtained from the project status report, and these projections provide new entries for the cost and schedule outlook reports.

For the propulsion system, the manager could determine that:

- As of the end of October 1961, the anticipated system completion was 1 week ahead of schedule, with a projected overrun of $100,000.
- As of the end of November, the outlook was for system completion in 4 weeks, ahead of schedule, but at a projected cost overrun of $200,000.
- By the end of January, both cost and schedule projections were significantly poorer.
- From the end of January to the end of March, the cost projections improved considerably, while the schedule projection deteriorated further and then showed slight improvement.

By relating the trend of these projections to previous management decisions, the manager can observe the effects of these decisions on cost and schedule for the project. He can determine, on a

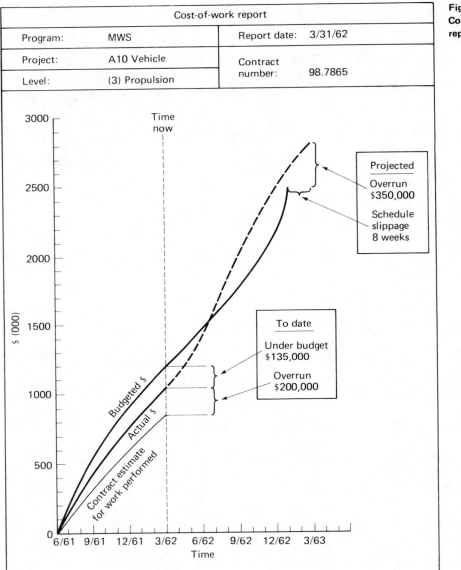

Figure 9–4.
Cost-of-work
report

Budgeted $ = planned rate of expenditure.
Actual $ = expenditures and commitments made to date.

Figure 9-5.
Cost outlook report

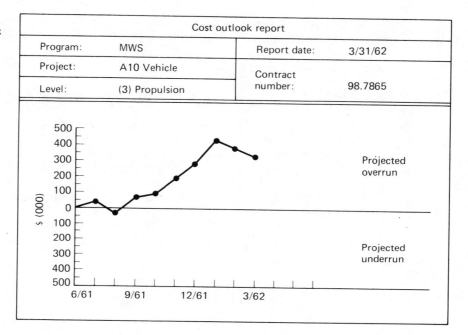

Figure 9-6.
Schedule outlook report

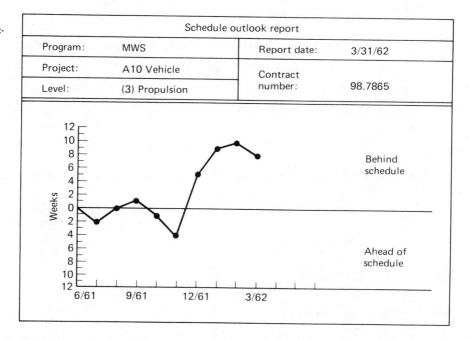

month-to-month basis, whether or not the actions taken to control schedules and costs are producing the desired results.

Milestone Reports

Selected PERT/COST network activities will represent major milestones of accomplishment toward project completion. It is quite useful to give additional project status guidance to management by reporting on these.

The milestones should be clearly identifiable in time. They should represent key network activities that are of major significance in achieving the project objectives.

The *milestone report* illustrated in Figure 9–7 shows the project manager:

- Each milestone scheduled during the current year of the program
- Action accomplished on schedule
- Action not accomplished on schedule
- Scheduled future action

The milestone report illustrated in Figure 9–8 shows the project manager:

- Each milestone scheduled during the life of the program
- The scheduled completion date for each milestone
- The expected completion date for each milestone
- The latest slack calculation results for each milestone
- When and where management action is required

THE PLANNING AND CONTROL CYCLE

The PERT/COST system can be represented as a cycle with two components: the planning cycle and the control cycle. This is shown in Figure 9–9.

Preparing the Project Work Breakdown Structure

By developing the work breakdown structure, we:

1. Define the project tasks to be performed and establish their relation to the project end item(s) and project objectives.

| | | | Fy 1961 | | | | | | Fy 1962 | | | | | | | | | |
| | | | Cy 1961 | | | | | | | | | | Cy 1962 | | | | |
Line	Milestones	J	F	M	A	M	J	J	A	S	O	N	D	J	F	M	A	M	J
1	Fuel quantity gaging				◆				⬆										
2																			
3	Engine PERT									⬆									
4																			
5	Complete R and D DEI							⬆											
6																			
7	Prototype delivered									◆⇧									
8																			
9	Letter contract award											⇧							
10																			
11	Material support plan											⇧							
12																			
13	PERT implementation												⇧						
14																			
15																			
16	Deliver 1st production article																⇧		
17																			
18	R and D testing ends																	⇧	
19																			
20																			
21																			
22																			
23																			
24																			
25																			
26																			
27																			
28																			
29																			
30																			
31																			
32																			
33																			

Current year milestone schedule

Reports control symbol
2APSC–R32

As of date
30 September 1961

Typed name and title of authenticator
FRANK J. NORTON, CAPT. USAF

Signature of authenticator
F. J. Norton

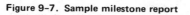

◆ Accomplished   ⬆ Past scheduled dates   ⇧ Future scheduled dates

Figure 9-7. Sample milestone report

171

Event	Slack (weeks)
Submit proto specification	−6.4
Approve proto specification	−6.4
Deliver mock-up	+2.2
Submit product specification	−6.3
Approve product specification	−6.3
Complete official proto PFRT	−6.7
Approve proto PFRT	−6.7
Deliver 1st proto hardware	−6.7
Deliver test hardware	−8.6

Date 1/24/61   Week 107.9

Timeline: J F M A M J J A S O N D (1961) J F M A M J J A S O N D (1962) J F M A M J J A S O N D (1963)

S = schedule.

E = earliest completion date.

M = management action.

Slack = degree of constraint to end schedule.

Figure 9–8. Sample milestone report

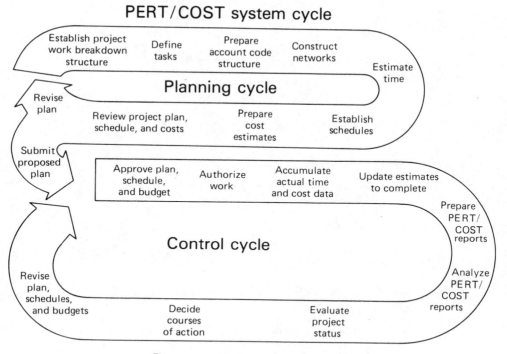

Figure 9-9. PERT/COST system cycle

2. Establish the framework for integrated cost and schedule planning and control.

3. Establish a framework for summarizing the cost and schedule status of the project for progressively higher levels of management.

The project work breakdown structure also serves as the basis for the PERT network of activities and events.

End Item Subdivision: The development of the work breakdown structure begins at the highest level of the project with the identification of the end items (hardware, services, equipment, facilities). The major end items are then divided into their component parts and the component parts are further subdivided into more detailed units (Figure 9-10). The subdivision continues to successively lower levels, reducing the dollar value and complexity of the units at each level, until it reaches the level where the end item subdivisions finally become manageable units for planning and control purposes. The end item subdivisions appearing at this last level are then divided into major work packages (e.g., engineering, manufacturing, testing) and responsibility is assigned to corresponding operating units.

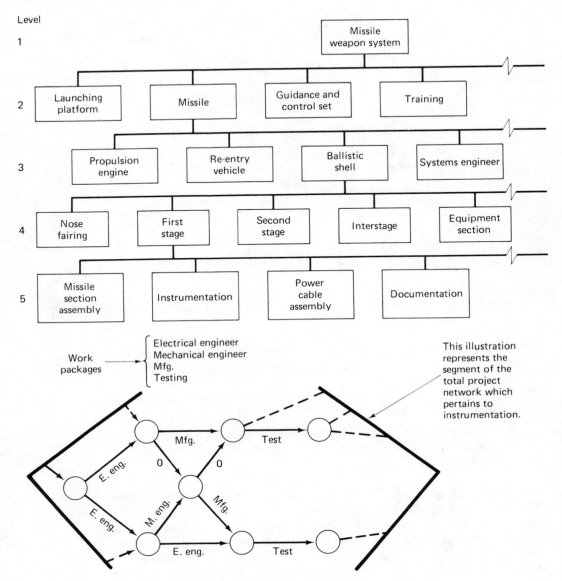

Figure 9-10. Simplified example of work breakdown structure

The end item subdivision "Ballistic Shell Instrumentation," appearing on the lowest level of the simplified work breakdown structure, requires engineering, manufacturing, and testing work (i.e., three major work packages are identified). The engineering work package is further divided into electrical and mechanical engineering—for assignment of responsibility and for cost and resource planning, and control—because of the complexity of work to be performed. Since the responsibility for manufacturing and testing effort rests with a single unit in the contractor's organization and the dollar value is small enough, these units could be treated as separate work packages.

The number of subdivisions depends on the dollar value of the major work packages and the detail needed to control the work. Normally, the lowest-level work packages represent a value of no more than $100,000 in cost and no more than 3 months in time.

In the example, the four work packages—electrical engineering, mechanical engineering, manufacturing, and testing—as identified in the end item subdivision "Instrumentation," constitute the basic units for estimating and accumulating costs.

Network Activities: Work packages at the lowest level are usually represented by a number of activities in the PERT network, separated by events which serve as beginning or ending points for other activities in the project. For example:

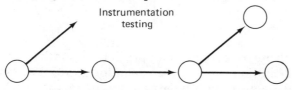

Instrumentation testing

Sometimes, however, a single activity with a beginning and ending event describes a work package. For example:

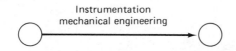

Instrumentation mechanical engineering

It is important to note that not all work packages will appear on the PERT network. In those cases where a work package is not directed toward a specific accomplishment of activities and events, the work need not be represented on the PERT network.

We can summarize the work breakdown structure as shown in Figure 9–11. The process does not have to occur in the exact order indicated, of course.

As the work progresses, the project work breakdown structure serves as the framework for summarizing data, so that the amount of detail presented at any level is commensurate with the decision-making requirements of management at that level.

The work packages formed at the lowest level of breakdown constitute the basic units in the PERT/COST system by which actual costs are collected.

The level of detail to which it is desirable to apply the PERT/COST system is largely a matter of judgment and varies from project

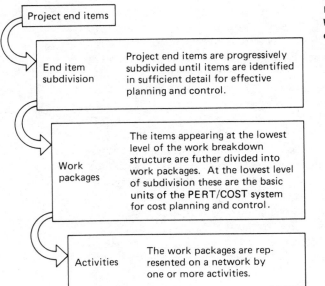

Figure 9-11.
Work break-
down structure

to project, from one part of a project to another, and from the proposal preparation stage to the execution stage of the same project. The level of detail should be a function of factors, such as the size and complexity of the project, the degree of uncertainty, the familiarity with the work to be performed, and the time available for planning.

Preparing the Account Code Structure

The *account code structure* is the framework of numbers used for charging and summarizing the project costs. *Summary numbers* are assigned to each item subdivision on the project work breakdown structure, and *charge numbers* are assigned to each of the work packages at the lowest level of subdivision (Figure 9-12). All costs are first collected or recorded under the charge numbers assigned to the work packages. The summary numbers are then used to group or summarize costs for each end item subdivision for use by progressively higher levels of project management.

The PERT/COST system does not require costs to be estimated for each activity on the network. This would just tend to generate expensive detail and fail to give proper weight to the relative cost significance of the various activities. Each cost activity constituting a work package is treated as a single unit for purposes of cost and resource planning and control. Again, the work package at the low-

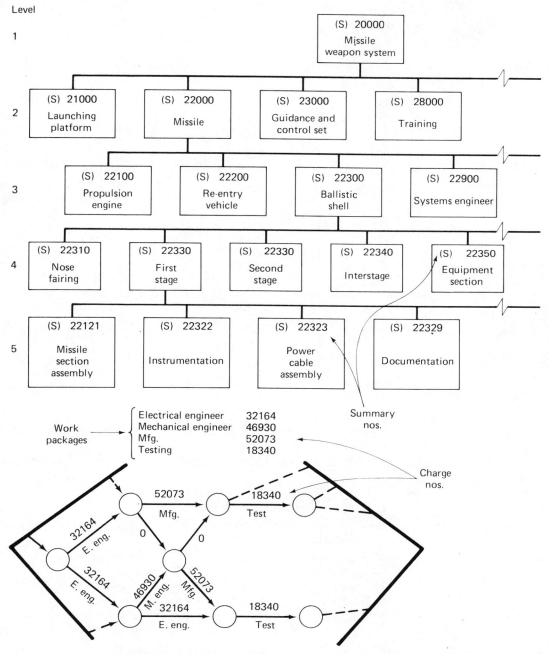

Figure 9–12. Simplified example of a work breakdown structure and account code structure

est level of subdivision is the basic unit, and all costs are collected under the same charge number.

OTHER REPORTS

Project Status Report

This report provides a summary of operations as well as detailed time and cost information. It is used to evaluate overall time and cost progress and to pinpoint areas contributing to schedule slippages and cost overruns (Figure 9–13). This information is summarized for each level of management with the summary items corresponding to the work breakdown structure.

Financial Plan and Status Report

The *financial plan and status report* assists in planning and controlling the rate of expenditure for the project (Figure 9–14). It summarizes, by future months, the total costs planned for each account. It also compares planned and actual total costs for current and past months.

UPDATING

As a project progresses, activities are added or deleted, work is completed behind or ahead of schedule, and time and cost estimates for unfinished work are revised. The PERT/COST system provides systematic *updating* by:

1. Establishing specific review dates.
2. Requiring the assignment of responsibility for estimate preparation and revision.
3. Supplying the current schedule and cost status to the individuals responsible for developing revised estimates.
4. Furnishing specific forms for transmittal of updated information.
5. Requiring reestimates when current information indicates changes in the initial estimates of personnel, material, and other resources necessary to perform the work.

Project status report

| Project: | Mark 93 ground support | Contract no. | 98.7865 | Report date: | 11/30/61 |

Identification					Time status				Cost status			
Charge or summary no.	Level*	Begin event no.	End event no.	Schedule elapsed time (weeks)	Date completed	Earliest completion date (S_E)	Latest completion date (S_L)	Activity slack (weeks) ($S_L - S_E$)	Actual to date $	Contract estimate $	Latest revised estimate $	Overrun (underrun) $
71831070	6	598	599	9.0	11/30/61	12/21/61	12/30/61	1.3	5,600	5,600	5,600	
71831072	6	601	602	1.0		05/03/62	03/30/62	-4.8		1,450	1,650	200
670057	5	590	602			05/03/62		-4.8	5,600	28,300	24,200	(4,100)
71831083		565	568	6.0		04/02/62	04/27/62	3.6				
		577	578	1.0		05/09/62	02/27/62	-1.7				
	6	565	578			05/09/62		-1.7	2,740	14,700	14,700	
670037	5	590	610			05/27/62		-1.7	129,000	660,000	657,900	(2,100)
670016	4	001	999			01/31/63		-4.8	889,000	3,640,000	3,665,200	25,200

*Summary level { 6. Charge level
5. Time and cost summary at major hardware level
4. Time and cost summary at subsystem level

Figure 9–13. Project status report

179

Financial plan and status report					
Project: Mark 93 ground support		Contract no. 98.7865		Report date: 12/30/61	
		Dollars			
Month	Charge no.	Actual to date	Contract estimate	Latest revised estimate	Over (under) plan
Cumulative Prior months	71831017 71834092	1,200 13,500	1,100 14,000	1,200 13,500	100 (500)
12/61	71831028 71834092	1,200 3,500 183,700*	1,200 3,100 183,300*	1,200 3,500 183,700*	400 400*
01/62	71831028 71834097 71834076 71831039		1,200 2,300 2,500 1,400	1,300 2,300 2,500 1,400	100
		889,000**	3,640,000**	3,675,000**	35,000**

Figure 9–14.
Financial plan and status report

* Total by month.

** Total for project.

PROJECT EVALUATION AND MANAGEMENT ACTION

Through a review of the output reports, the status of the project can be determined. Based on these evaluations, the project manager can take several actions to minimize costs and avoid schedule slippages. The manager can:

- Adjust the schedule of slack path activities to minimize the need for overtime or additional hiring.
- Reallocate funds from areas of underrun to more critical areas.
- Revise the planned resources for more packages by:
  — Trading off interchangeable resources between critical and slack path activities.
  — Increasing or reducing the planned resources.

- Revise network sequence or content by:
  - —Employing a greater or lesser amount of concurrence in performing activities.
  - —Modifying the specifications or method of performing the work.

SUMMARY

The material covered in this session is summarized in the following under proposal preparation, negotiation, project execution, and the project evaluation.

A. Proposal Preparation

1. Define the project objectives in terms of the project end items.
2. Prepare a project work breakdown structure showing successively further subdivisions of the project end items into functional work packages, then into activities.
3. Construct a PERT network of activities and events showing the dependency and precedence relations imposed by the technical nature of the work.
4. Prepare elapsed time estimates for each network activity based on a normal or anticipated level of resources.
5. Calculate and/or identify:
   a. Critical path.
   b. Slack paths.
6. Print out the basic PERT reports and compare the calculated completion dates with the directed completion dates.
7. Revise the network, if required to meet any direct completion dates, by any or all of the following methods:
   a. Revise the network configuration to reflect a greater or lesser amount of concurrence in performing activities.
   b. Apply a greater or lesser level of effort in performing activities.
   c. Modify the technical approach by altering, deleting, and/or adding activities.
   d. Recycle steps A–4 through A–6, where necessary.
   e. Establish activity schedules.
8. Develop an account code structure conforming to the work breakdown structure in step A–2.
9. Assign charge numbers to the work packages at the lowest-level subdivision and summary numbers to all end items appearing on the project work breakdown structure.

10. Estimate, for each charge account, the labor-hours by individual or composite skills and by months required to accomplish the work in the scheduled duration as determined in step A-7e.

11. Develop an estimated dollar cost projection for each charge account. This estimate should include:
    a. Labor costs.
    b. Material and subcontract costs.
    c. Special equipment, services, and other direct costs.
    d. Indirect costs where overhead percentage rates apply.

12. Calculate:
    a. Consolidated labor-hour requirements by months and by labor skills, showing activities with positive slack and those with negative slack occurring during the same month.
    b. A financial plan by months, including any indirect costs not accounted for in step A-11d.

13. Successively higher levels of management evaluate the plan:
    a. Determine that personnel and other resource requirements are consistent with availability.
    b. Determine whether idle resources and premium costs could be reduced by adjusting slack path activities.

14. Revise network plans, if required by management review, to improve labor loading and the outlook for meeting schedules:
    a. Adjust the schedule for activities on slack paths within the limits of the earliest completion dates and the latest allowable completion dates.
    b. Revise the planned level of resources for work packages:
       (1) Trade off interchangeable resources between critical and slack path activities, and/or
       (2) Increase or reduce the resources planned for specific activities.
    c. Revise the network configuration to reflect a greater or lesser amount of concurrence in performing activities.
    d. Modify the technical approach or reduce the performance requirements by altering and/or deleting, and/or adding activities.
    e. Recycle steps A-5, A-12, and A-13, if necessary.

15. Approve schedules and budgets for the project.

16. Incorporate the schedules, budgets, and related networks into the proposed plan.

B. Negotiation

1. Reaffirm or revise technical specifications and time and cost information to meet project requirements.

2. Recycle steps A-1 through A-15 to reflect any revised project requirements.

3. Contract awarded and work authorized to begin.

C. Project Execution

1. Charge actual labor, material, and other direct costs to account charge numbers according to normal company procedures.
2. Summarize actual cost data by the summary numbers developed in step A–9.
3. Record work progress in terms of completed activities.
4. Prepare revised time and cost estimates-to-complete for work-in-progress or work not yet started which cannot be completed within the original estimates.
5. Periodically process actual costs and schedule data and revised estimates-to-complete for preparation of PERT/COST reports.

D. Project Evaluation

1. Print out the project status report:
   a. For completed work, print out:
      (1) Actual completion dates.
      (2) Actual costs, estimated costs, and overruns/underruns.
   b. For work-in-process, print out:
      (1) Earliest schedule completion dates, latest schedule completion dates, and positive or negative slack.
      (2) Estimated contract costs, actual costs to date, latest revised estimates, and anticipated cost overruns/underruns.
   c. For work not yet started, print out the latest revisions of:
      (1) Earliest schedule completion dates, latest schedule completion dates, and positive or negative slack.
      (2) Contract estimated costs, latest revised estimates, and predicted cost overruns/underruns.
2. Print out other PERT/COST reports:
   a. Operating unit status report
   b. Financial plan and status report
   c. Labor loading report
3. Prepare PERT/COST management reports:
   a. PERT/COST management summary
   b. Labor loading report and display
   c. Cost-of-work report
   d. Schedule and cost outlook reports
   e. Delivery dates for each deliverable item
4. Successively higher levels of management evaluate output reports.
5. Revise the current plan, if necessary, to avoid or minimize predicted cost overruns and/or scheduled slippages by:
   a. Adjusting the schedule of slack path activities.
   b. Revising the planned levels of resources for functional work packages.
      (1) Trade off interchangeable resources between critical and slack path activities.

        (2) Increase or reduce the planned resources for activities.

    c. Revising network sequence and/or content:

        (1) Employ a greater or lesser amount of concurrence in performing the activities of the network.

        (2) Modify the technical specifications, if permissible, to allow deletion and/or addition of activities to the network.

6. Recycle steps A-5, A-12, and A-13.

7. Submit summarized cost and schedule reports.

Definitions

Activities: Project work items having specific beginning and completion points, and duration times.

Activities List: A list of the project work items with accompanying descriptions which are used in preparing the network plan.

Arrow: A line with an arrowhead depicting an activity. The arrow shows direction and the passage of time.

Arrow Diagram: A graphic diagram of arrows representing component jobs and the manner in which they are connected, depicting the interrelationship among project jobs. An arrow diagram is the same as a network diagram.

Bar Chart: A chart with time activities shown as rectangular bars. The length of each bar shows duration, and the position of each bar indicates when the activity will be scheduled. May also be called a Gantt Chart, named after its developer, Henry Gantt.

Basic: A conversational programming language that permits the use of simple English words, abbreviations, and familiar mathematical symbols to perform logical and arithmetical operations.

Branching: An arrow diagramming error caused by two activities using the same unique designations.

Cash Flow: The income and disbursements during the span of a project.

COBOL: An acronym for COmmon Business-Oriented Language; a language formed by commonly used English nouns, verbs, and connectives, and designed specifically for application to commercial data processing problems.

Computer Hardware: The physical elements of a computer.

Computer Printout: Computer output in printed form to be used for analysis.

Computer Program: The set of instructions in computer language used by the computer to make necessary calculations.

Computer Software: The programs used to instruct the computer to perform its operations.

Cost Estimate: An estimate of cost to complete a project job based upon the resources used to accomplish the job.

Cost Slope: The rate of cost increase per unit of time duration of a work item. For example, to determine the rate of cost increase to expedite a job:

$$\text{Cost slope} = \frac{\text{Crash cost} - \text{Normal cost}}{\text{Normal duration} - \text{Crash duration}}$$

Crash Cost: The estimated cost for a job based on its crash time.

Crash Duration: The minimal time in which a job may be completed by expediting the work.

Critical Activity: A project work item on the critical path having zero float time.

Critical Path: The longest continuous path of activities through a network diagram from beginning to end of a project. The total time elapsed on the critical path, which will have zero total float, is the shortest duration of the project.

CPM (Critical Path Method): A network planning technique that is activity-oriented (utilizing arrow diagramming), used for planning and scheduling a project.

Direct Cost: The portion of the total cost that is directly related to the time in which a project item is completed. Labor costs are direct costs.

Dummy Arrow: A dashed arrow used in a network to show relationships among project items. A dummy or dummy arrow requires no time nor resources.

Duration: Activity duration is the estimated time required to complete a project job. Project duration is the total time required to complete the project as determined by the critical path. The time units may be in hours, days, or months.

Earliest Finish Time: The earliest possible time an activity can be completed without interfering with the completion of any of the preceding activites.

Earliest Start Time: The earliest possible time an activity can begin without interfering with the completion of any of the preceding activities.

Elapsed Time: The actual time required to accomplish a job in the project. Time may be measured in days, weeks, or any unit of time that is consistently considered through the project. Elapsed time used in network planning analysis includes the total length of time between the beginning and end of a project job item.

Event: A point in time shown as a circle at a junction of arrows in the network plan. It may also indicate a milestone of the completion of preceding project items. In CPM, an event is more commonly stated as a node.

Expected Time: The weighted average of the estimated optimistic, most likely, and pessimistic duration times to perform a project activity:

$$\text{Expected time} = \frac{\text{Optimistic} + 4(\text{Most likely}) + \text{Pessimistic}}{6}$$

Float: The amount of time a project job can be delayed without affecting the duration of the project. Total float is the difference between the time that is calculated to be available for a work item to be completed and the estimated duration time of that work item.

FORTRAN: An acronym for FORmula TRANslator; a computer language that uses common scientific expressions and notations in its vocabulary.

Free Float: The amount of time a designated activity can be delayed without affecting the succeeding activities.

i and j: Symbols designating the origin and terminal nodes, respectively, for an activity. For computer use, each activity is unique and needs to be defined by an (i, j) designation.

Independent Float: The amount of time an activity can be delayed without affecting the earliest start of the preceding activity and the latest finish of the succeeding activity.

Indirect Cost: Costs that are not associated directly with time in completing the activity. Overhead and insurance are indirect costs.

Input: Data prepared for use into a computer system.

Latest Finish Time: The latest time an activity must be completed without delaying the end of the project.

Latest Start Time: The latest time an activity can start without delaying the end of the project.

Leeway (time): Same as Float (time).

Logic Diagram: The network plan without time estimates, showing the interrelationships of project activities.

Looping: An arrow diagramming error caused by an arrow in reverse direction in the network diagram.

Management by Exception: A technique that signals problems that require the manager's attention.

Management by Objectives: A technique that defines objectives and arranges a discipline procedure to measure performance against the planned objectives.

Milestone: A major event in the project. These events may be designated as important delivery dates, major phase of building construction completion, or equipment installation completion.

Network Plan: The graphic analysis of a project, showing the plan of action through the use of a graphic diagram of arrows. *See also* Arrow Diagram.

Node: Shown graphically in the network plan as a circle depicting the beginning or end of an activity. A node represents an instantaneous point in time and occurs at the junction of arrows.

Normal Cost: The estimate of the direct cost for a project job to be performed in a normal time.

Normal Time: The estimated job time to be performed at a normal cost.

PERT (Program Evaluation and Review Technique): An event-oriented network diagramming technique used for planning and scheduling.

Project: An undertaking having a definite objective, and specific beginning and completion points. The breakdown of the work items that comprise the project are set up in a logical order to achieve the objective.

Project Control: The third phase of the project management cycle that compares the actual performance of the project activites with the planned schedule, and taking corrective action, where required, to avoid delays.

Project Costs Chart: A graph showing the disbursements, both plan and actual, over the length of the project.

Project Plan: The initial phase of project management, where, after setting objectives, the plan of action is developed into a logical order and portrayed in an arrow diagram.

Resource: Money, skills, personnel, material, or equipment that may be utilized in completing a project.

Resource Allocation: Assignment of resources to each project activity.

Resource Levelling: The method of scheduling activities within their available float times so as to minimize fluctuations in day-to-day resource requirements.

Schedule: The second phase of the project management cycle, detailing the time at which every job is to be started and completed. The times assigned for starting and completing activities are predicated on the float calculations of the project items.

Simulation: A management technique using the work plan to evaluate alternative plans to determine the best project schedule.

Slack: Used in a PERT network to show the difference between the latest allowable finish time and the earliest possible starting time of a given event. Has the same analogy as float in the CPM network.

Status Report: A communication expedient in the project control phase to inform management on the status of the project.

Time/Cost Trade-offs: A scheduling technique by which the project duration is shortened with a minimum of added costs.

Total Cost: The sum of direct and indirect costs for a work activity and/or the total project.

Total Float: The amount of time a project work item can be delayed without affecting the duration of the project. Total float time can be used in only one activity in a path.

Variance: Refers to deviations from normal costs, normal time, normal labor available, and so on.

Appendix

I. PROJECT REPORT

A few of the problems relate to projects that are carried through each of the chapters and may be used to prepare a term project report. Dividing the class into groups of three to five students for the workshop sessions is timely immediately after the discussions of the illustrative problems in Chapter 2.

Each group should have similar educational interests and/or work experiences as the selection of the particular workshop project problem should be compatible with each group's background. The project problem will develop through each chapter until a complete report evolves illustrating the effective methods for planning, scheduling, and controlling a project.

Each student, upon completion of this term project report, will have excellent reference material for future application. The project report is an excellent communication in business, government, and industry with management as it includes all of the elements of project management and arranges them in such a manner as to show an effective plan of action.

The term project contents may be outlined as follows:

    A. Letter of Transmittal

B. Table of Contents

C. Introduction

D. Summary

E. Project Management Report

    1. Statement(s) of the objective
    2. List of activities with descriptions
    3. Activity groupings
    4. Subdiagram
    5. Arrow diagram, including:
       a. Time estimates
       b. Earliest start times
       c. Latest finish times
       d. Critical path
    6. Total float tabulation
    7. Schedule tabulation
    8. Bar chart schedule
    9. Cost schedule
       a. Cost slope tabulation
       b. Cost expenditure schedule tabulation
       c. Indicated cost outcome
  10. Labor schedule
       a. Labor allocation (earliest start times)
          1. Tabulation
          2. Bar chart schedule with required labor
       b. Labor leveling
          1. Tabulation
          2. Revised bar chart schedule with leveled labor
       c. Labor load charts
          1. Earliest start
          2. After leveling

F. Appendix

    1. Handout material
    2. Calculations
    3. Computer printouts

As the techniques of report writing is a course in itself, we will not attempt to offer any thorough instructions on its preparation. However, writing reports becomes an important part of a project manager's responsibilities. It may be the main line of communication. The degree to which he can develop his communication line will provide a measure of his success, not only with his relationship to members of management, but with the project itself. When communication with management has been accomplished, it is a good sign that communication with all the other members associated with the project has also been realized.

The following notes on some of the key elements of a project report may be helpful to those writing a report:

INTRODUCTION: The introduction should briefly describe the *Purpose* (a statement of the problem), *Scope* (boundary of the problem), *Limits* (money, time, design, criteria, labor, etc.), and *Background* (facts behind the project). A report may or may not include all of the above in the introduction; however, in some instances they may be combined.

A two or three paragraph introduction is usually adequate. It is advisable to review the introduction after completing the other sections of the report as the scope may have been enlarged. Refining the complete introduction is also recommended upon completion of the report.

SUMMARY: The summary presents the entire work on approximately one typewritten page. In recent years this page has been titled *highlights* or *executive highlights* and is made up of numbered or bullet (•) statements. Almost all of its contents will be the decisions and judgments (also known as conclusions and recommendations) based on the findings given in the report.

Place the summary (or *highlights*) immediately after the introduction as it has a better chance of being read. Management usually has a greater interest in what the report has accomplished rather than the method in which the findings were made.

CONCLUSIONS: Conclusions are the primary reason the report is written; prepare clear, concise, and direct statements and arrange them in some order. While conclusions and recommendations may be combined, it should be recognized that each recommendation is derived from one or more of the conclusions. Therefore, each recommendation must have some support from the conclusions. Whenever possible, provide alternate courses of action, or options, and a preferred approach.

DESCRIPTION (*Project Management Report*): The description is the main body of the report and should represent the "meat" of the report — what was done, how it was done, and what the solutions were.

The narrative portions of the body of the report are usually written in the third person — we, they, etc. Use headings and subheadings to organize the material into categories of information. (The report outline represents a good reference for headings and subheading titles.)

APPENDIX: The appendix is a collection of explanatory material which cannot be given in the body of the report without disturbing its logical development. The appendix includes calculations, reference literature, supportive charts, and any other notes that do not pertain directly to the report.

Wherever possible, place detailed data in the appendix. Place detailed diagrams as near the initial reference as possible.

II. TEXT PROBLEMS

Chapter 1

1. Define the following project management principles:
   a. Network analysis
   b. Management by objectives
   c. Management by exception
   d. Cost scheduling
   e. Cost minimizing
   f. Resource allocation
   g. Resource leveling

2. A project management cycle consists of three major phases. Identify them and provide a brief definition of each.

3. Prepare a tabulation showing advantages and disadvantages of bar charts or Gantt charts. Do the same for the network diagramming method.

4. What are the differences between the critical path method (CPM) and project evaluation review technique (PERT) methods of network diagramming?

Chapter 2

1. Draw a diagram for the following:
   Project consists of five Jobs: A, B, C, D, and E.
   At project start, Jobs A and B can begin.
   Job C follows Job A (only).
   Job D follows A and B.
   Job E follows Jobs B and C.
   When Jobs D and E are finished, the project is complete.

2. Develop a network diagram for the following projects where the major project jobs have been defined:
   a. Theater planning: The activities are listed below in a random fashion. There may be differences of opinion on the sequence to be used to arrive at "opening night."

(1) Form organization	(8) Conduct publicity campaign
(2) Complete financing	(9) Conduct rehearsals
(3) Select play	(10) Conduct dress rehearsals
(4) Contact stars	(11) Book out-of-town shows
(5) Select director	(12) Procure scenery
(6) Select cast	(13) Conduct out-of-town shows
(7) Select set designer	(14) Prepare for opening night

b. Changing a flat tire: Assume that there are four people in the car who can help in changing the tire.

(1) Remove flat	(13) Open trunk
(2) Remove lugs	(14) Replace lugs
(3) Get lug wrench	(15) Put flat in car
(4) Get spare tire	(16) Get screwdriver
(5) Remove hubcap	(17) Lower car
(6) Get jack	(18) Replace jack
(7) Position jack	(19) Close trunk
(8) Loosen lugs	(20) Replace wrench
(9) Stop car	(21) Drive off safely
(10) Replace screwdriver	(22) Replace hubcap
(11) Jack-up car	(23) Tighten lugs
(12) Put on spare	

c. Getting Dad ready for work: Dad, Mother, and the two children help Dad to arrive at work as efficiently as possible. Listed below are a group of activities, and whether they are performed by Dad (D), Mother (M), or the children (C):

(1) Set alarm	(D)		(9) Eat breakfast	(D)
(night before)			(10) Put dishes in sink	(C)
(2) Awake to alarm	(D)		(11) Put on hat and coat	(D)
(3) Wash	(D)		(12) Wake wife	(D)
(4) Shave	(D)		(13) Wake kids	(D)
(5) Dress	(D)		(14) Start car and warm	
(6) Set table	(C)		up	(D)
(7) Fry eggs	(M)		(15) Kiss wife goodbye	(D)
(8) Make coffee	(M)		(16) Drive to work	(D)

3. (For Industrial Supervision students): You are required to move your production operation from the existing location to a new plant 25 miles away. Develop a plan to make the move with minimum lost production time.
   - All of the existing equipment will be reinstalled.
   - There are two similar production lines and they will be reinstalled.

4. (For Engineering students): Your architectural engineering firm has been chosen to prepare designs and specifications for a large building project. Develop a plan for identifying the responsibilities of the civil, electrical, and mechanical engineering departments to implement this project.

5. (For Computer Systems students): As systems manager of a manufacturing firm, you are assigned the task of developing a plan for an information system. Prepare a simple diagram showing the major activities in developing such a system.

6. Prepare a sample network of ten to fifteen jobs for constructing a house. (Include such major activities as constructing foundation, framing, siding, millwork, electrical, plumbing, build and paint walls, decorate interior, and landscaping.)

Chapter 3

1. Given the network diagrams, compute the earliest start and latest finish times, and total float. Locate the critical path on the network diagrams.
   a. Lawn project (Students to estimate durations)
      1. One-person job (Figure A-1)
      2. Two-person job (Figure A-2)
   b. Changing a flat tire (Figure A-4)
   c. Getting Dad ready for work (Figure A-5)
   d. Theater planning (Figure A-3)
   e. New equipment installation (Figure A-6)

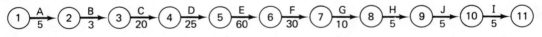

Figure A-1. Lawn-mowing project: one-person job

Figure A-2.
Lawn-mowing
project: two-
person job

A Procure tools
B Trash barrel to job sites
C Mow lawn parimeter
D Clip edges
E Mow lawn

F Rake clippings
G Dump clippings
H Empty catcher
I Return tools
J Return trash barrel

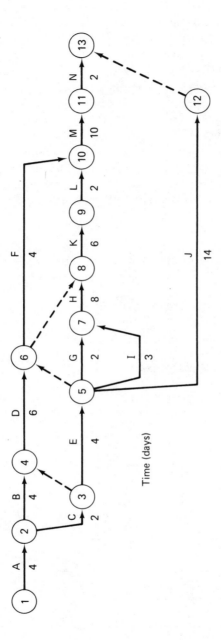

A 1, 2   Form organization
B 2, 4   Complete financing
C 2, 3   Select play
D 4, 6   Contract stars
E 3, 5   Select director
F 6, 10 Book out-of-town shows
G 5, 7   Select set designer

H 7, 8   Procure scenery props
I 5, 8   Select cast
J 5, 12 Conduct publicity campaign
K 8, 9   Conduct rehearsals
L 9, 10 Conduct dress rehearsals
M 10, 11 Out-of-town shows
N 11, 12 Opening night preparations

Time (days)

Figure A–3. Theater planning

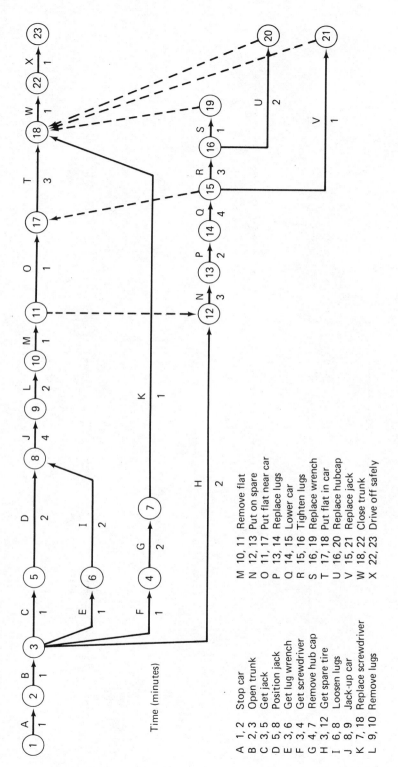

Figure A–4. Changing a flat tire; four-person job

A 1, 2   Stop car
B 2, 3   Open trunk
C 3, 5   Get jack
D 5, 8   Position jack
E 3, 6   Get lug wrench
F 3, 4   Get screwdriver
G 4, 7   Remove hub cap
H 3, 12   Get spare tire
I 6, 8   Loosen lugs
J 8, 9   Jack-up car
K 7, 18   Replace screwdriver
L 9, 10   Remove lugs

M 10, 11   Remove flat
N 12, 13   Put on spare
O 11, 17   Put flat near car
P 13, 14   Replace lugs
Q 14, 15   Lower car
R 15, 16   Tighten lugs
S 16, 19   Replace wrench
T 17, 18   Put flat in car
U 16, 20   Replace hubcap
V 15, 21   Replace jack
W 18, 22   Close trunk
X 22, 23   Drive off safely

Time (minutes)

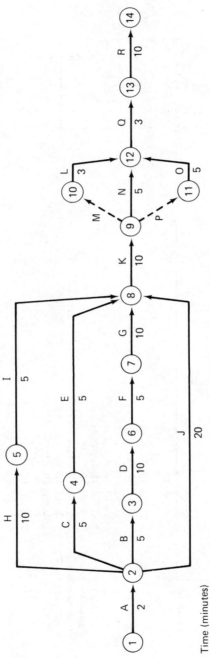

A 1, 2 Set alarm
B 2, 3 Awake to alarm
C 2, 4 Wake wife
D 3, 6 Wash
E 4, 8 Fry eggs
F 6, 7 Shave
G 7, 8 Dress
H 2, 6 Wake kids
I 6, 8 Set table

J 2, 8 Make coffee
K 8, 9 Eat breakfast
L 10, 12 Put dishes in sink
M 9, 10 Dummy
N 9, 12 Put on hat and coat
O 11, 12 Start car and warm up
P 9, 11 Dummy
Q 12, 13 Kiss wife
R 13, 14 Drive to work

Time (minutes)

Figure A-5. Getting Dad to work

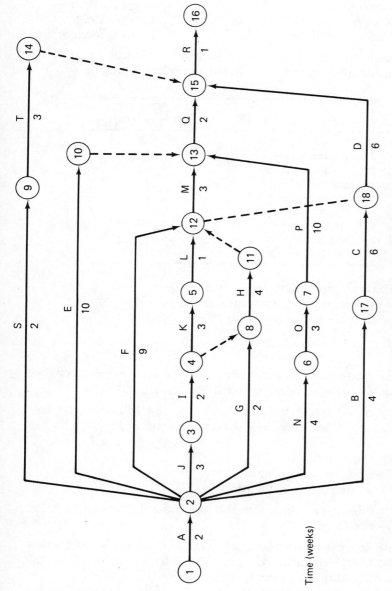

Time (weeks)

A 1, 2   Design equipment
B 2, 17   Design building
C 17, 18 Construct building – phase I
D 18, 15 Construct building – phase II
E 2, 10   Procure long-lead equipment items
F 2, 12   Procure ancillary equipment
G 2, 8   Remove existing equipment
H 8, 11   Prepare site
I 3, 4   Design equipment installation
J 2, 3   Detail equipment

K 4, 5   Fabricate equipment (shop)
L 5, 12   Assemble equipment (shop)
M 12, 13 Install – phase I
N 2, 6   Design controls
O 6, 7   Select controls supplier
P 7, 13   Fabricate and assemble controls
Q 13, 15 Install – phase II
R 15, 16 Debug equipment
S 2, 9   Develop operating procedures
T 9, 14   Select and train personnel

Figure A-6. New equipment installation

199

2. For each of the projects in Problem 1, complete a work sheet showing schedule information as follows:

   a. Job
   b. Description
   c. Duration
   d. Earliest start time
   e. Earliest finish time
   f. Latest start time
   g. Latest finish time
   h. Total float
   i. Free float
   j. Independent float

3. Refurnishing an office — The following activities must be accomplished to complete an office remodeling project:

Activity	Estimated duration (days)
Procure paint	2
Procure new carpet	5
Procure new furniture	7
Remove old furniture	1
Remove old carpet	1
Scrub walls	1
Paint walls	2
Lay new carpet	1
Move in new furniture	1

   a. Draw an arrow diagram for this project.
   b. When can the new furniture be moved in?
   c. What is the project duration?

Chapter 4

1. Draw a bar chart time schedule for the lawn-mowing project using two people. See Chapter 3, Problem 1a(2).

2. Draw a bar chart time schedule for the following projects whose schedules were developed in Chapter 3, Problem 2:
   a. Theater planning
   b. Changing a flat tire
   c. Getting dad ready for work
   d. New equipment installation

3. Draw a bar chart time schedule for the computer installation project in Chapter 7.

4. Show the status on the bar chart time schedule of the new equipment installation project in its 12th week, reflecting the following progress of the work activities:

   - Prepare detail equipment   Behind 2 weeks
   - Prepare site   Behind 4 weeks
   - Fabricate equipment (in shop)   Behind 2 weeks
   - Assemble equipment (in shop)   Behind 2 weeks
   - All other work activities are progressing as planned.

Does present status indicate an extension of the present project duration? If so, show on bar chart.

5. Repeat Problem 4 for the computer installation project in its 20th week.
   - Procure computer   Behind 3 weeks
   - Prepare site   Behind 2 weeks
   - Develop program   Behind 2 weeks
   - Procure forms   Behind 2 weeks
   - Design forms   Behind 2 weeks
   - All other work activities are progressing as planned.

6. Refer to Figure 4-2, the summary bar chart for the product introduction project. Show the status of this project on this chart in the 15th week.
   - Design package and set up facility   Behind 3 weeks
   - Order stock   Behind 2 weeks
   - Plan and conduct advertising campaign Behind 4 weeks
   - Hire and train sales personnel   Behind 3 weeks

Chapter 5

1. Prepare a cost schedule for the new equipment installation project (Chapter 4, Problem 1d).

New equipment installation

Activity	Cost (000)
Design equipment	$ 2.0
Prepare equipment design detail	5.4
Prepare equipment installation drawings	1.0
Remove existing equipment	5.0
Prepare site	20.0
Design building	20.0
Construct building — phase I	150.0
Construct building — phase II	85.0
Fabricate equipment (in shop)	15.0
Procure ancillary equipment	54.0
Procure long-lead equipment items	60.0
Assemble equipment (in shop)	10.0
Install equipment — phase I	12.0
Install equipment — phase II	8.0
Develop operating procedures	2.0
Select and train personnel	3.0
Debug equipment	3.0
Develop and design automatic controls	1.6
Select controls supplier	1.2
Fabricate and assemble controls package	25.0
Total	$483.2

2. Prepare a cost schedule for the computer installation project (Chapter 4, Problem 3).

Computer installation

Activity	Cost
Decide on computer	$ 3,200
Procure computer	100,000
Install and test computer	9,000
Determine site specifications	800
Solicit bids for site preparation	2,000
Award contract for site preparation	800
Prepare site	66,000
Select programming personnel	1,600
Select operating personnel	800
Train programming personnel	8,000
Train operating personnel	8,000
Layout computer records	2,000
Develop computer program	24,000
Test computer program	5,400
Design forms	2,000
Procure forms	2,000
Put program into operation	2,400
Total	$238,000

3. Reduce the project duration at minimum cost, one week at a time, until it is fully crashed (Figure A-7).

4. Boat Repair: The network diagram in Figure A-8 shows that it will require 14 days to complete the boat repair. The owner

Cost slope calculations
(additional cost/week reduced)

Job	Normal time	Crash time	Cost slope
1,2	4	4	–
1,3*	5	3	750
1,7	15	12	800
2,4	10	9	1,500
3,4*	10	6	500
3,5	10	8	1,500
4,6*	10	8	1,500
5,6	9	7	2,000
6,7*	5	3	1,000

*Critical path.

a. Complete the direct cost table.

Project duration (weeks)	Normal cost	Job(s) crashed	Weeks reduced	Crash cost	Total direct costs (normal and crash)
30	$38,000			$	$38,000
29		3,4	1	500	38,500
28		6,7	1	1,000	39,500
27					
26					
25					
24					

Figure A-7.

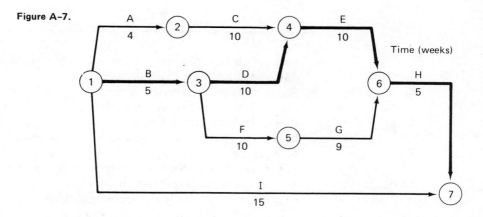

Job	Latest finish	Earliest start	Duration (weeks)	Total float
1, 2	5	0	4	1
*1, 3	5	5	5	0
1, 7	30	0	15	15
2, 4	15	4	10	1
*3, 4	15	5	10	0
3, 5	16	5	10	1
*4, 6	25	15	10	0
5, 6	25	15	9	1
*6, 7	30	25	5	0

*Critical path items.

of the boat had decided that he does not wish to be without the boat for 14 days and therefore is concerned with reducing the total time required for the project. He then obtains "crash" time and cost for the jobs in the project. The total normal times and costs as well as crash times and costs are tabulated below:

| Job | Normal data | | Crash data | |
	Time (days)	Cost	Time (days)	Cost
1,2	2	$ 0	1	$ 20
1,4*	10	200	6	240
2,3	3	150	2	750
3,4	2	0	1	20
4,5*	4	0	4	0

*Critical path.

a. Reduce the normal project duration at minimum cost one day at a time until it is fully crashed.

b. Suppose that the owner decides he cannot do without the boat while the craft is being repaired; as a result, he must determine the cost of hiring a boat. After checking several boat liveries, he finds that a suitable boat can be rented for $15 per day.

(1) What is the total minimum cost for the boat repair project if it is fully crashed?

(2) What is the *total* minimum cost for each day that the project duration is reduced between the normal and crash times?

The following format may be helpful:

| Project duration (days) | Jobs reduced | Normal cost | + | Extra cost | + | Cost of hiring a substitute boat | = | Total cost |

5. For the new product introduction project, reduce the duration of the project at minimum cost, one week at a time, until it is fully crashed (Figure A–9).

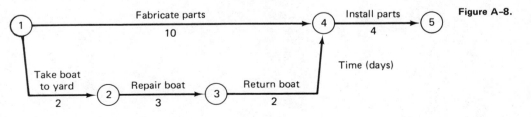

Figure A-8.

204

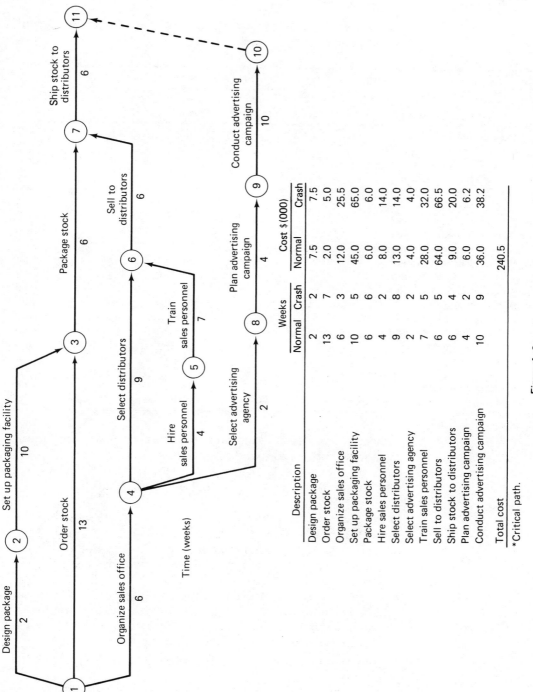

Description	Weeks		Cost $(000)	
	Normal	Crash	Normal	Crash
Design package	2	2	7.5	7.5
Order stock	13	7	2.0	5.0
Organize sales office	6	3	12.0	25.5
Set up packaging facility	10	5	45.0	65.0
Package stock	6	6	6.0	6.0
Hire sales personnel	4	2	8.0	14.0
Select distributors	9	8	13.0	14.0
Select advertising agency	2	2	4.0	4.0
Train sales personnel	7	5	28.0	32.0
Sell to distributors	6	5	64.0	66.5
Ship stock to distributors	6	4	9.0	20.0
Plan advertising campaign	4	2	6.0	6.2
Conduct advertising campaign	10	9	36.0	38.2
Total cost			240.5	

*Critical path.

Figure A-9.

6. Given below are the schedule and cost data for an equipment installation project:

Job description	Normal data		Crash data	
	Time (weeks)	Cost (000)	Time (weeks)	Cost (000)
Design equipment	2	$ 2.0	1	$ 4.0
Prepare equipment design detail	3	5.4	2	10.8
Prepare equipment installation drawings	2	1.0	2	1.0
Remove existing equipment	2	5.0	1	12.0
Prepare site	2	20.0	2	20.0
Design building	4	20.0	3	28.0
Construct building — phase I	6	150.0	4	200.0
Construct building — phase II	6	85.0	4	140.0
Fabricate equipment (in shop)	3	15.0	2	25.0
Procure ancillary equipment	9	54.0	8	70.0
Procure long-lead equipment items	10	60.0	7	80.0
Assemble equipment (in shop)	1	10.0	1	10.0
Install equipment — phase I	3	12.0	2	18.0
Install equipment — phase II	2	8.0	2	8.0
Develop operating procedures	2	2.0	1	3.5
Select and train personnel	3	3.0	2	5.0
Debug equipment	1	3.0	1	3.0
Develop and design automatic controls	4	1.6	3	2.5
Select controls supplier	3	1.2	2	2.0
Fabricate and assemble controls package	10	25.0	8	34.0

Indicated cost data, including the cost of lost production, insurance, supervision, and so on are as follows:

Total indirect cost for project duration = $100,000

Determine the minimum additional cost when reducing the project duration time by 6 weeks.

a. Arrive at the solutions by finding the cost slope for each work item and determine indirect and direct costs for the project at 2-week intervals.

b. Prepare a graph plotting project times on the horizontal line against project costs on the vertical side. Show direct costs, indirect costs, and total costs for a reduction of 6 weeks in project time in weekly increments.

7. Repeat Problem 6 for the computer installation project.

Total indirect cost for project duration = $20,000

| Job description | Normal data | | Crash data | |
	Time (weeks)	Cost (000)	Time (weeks)	Cost (000)
Decide on computer	4	$ 3.2	3	$ 4.4
Procure computer	25	100.0	21	120.0
Install and test computer	3	9.0	2	13.5
Determine site specifications	1	0.8	1	0.8
Solicit bids for site preparation	5	2.0	3	3.0
Award contract for site preparation	2	0.8	2	0.8
Prepare site	20	66.0	16	86.0
Select programming personnel	2	1.6	2	1.6
Select operating personnel	1	0.8	1	0.8
Train programming personnel	8	8.0	8	8.0
Train operating personnel	8	8.0	8	8.0
Layout computer records	2	2.0	2	2.0
Develop computer program	12	24.0	8	36.0
Test computer program	3	5.4	3	5.4
Design forms	2	2.0	2	2.0
Procure forms	2	2.0	2	2.0
Put program into operation	2	2.4	1	4.0

Chapter 6

1. Given below are the labor data for the new equipment installation project:

Labor allocation*

| Job description | Workers per week | | | | | |
	DR	D	ENG	E	P	L
Design equipment		4				
Prepare equipment design detail	6					
Prepare equipment installation drawings		2				
Remove existing equipment			1			6
Prepare site			1	2	4	
Design building	6		4			
Construct building — phase I			1	4	4	8
Construct building — phase II			1	6	6	4
Fabricate equipment (in shop)		1				
Procure ancillary equipment		2				
Procure long-lead equipment items		2				
Assemble equipment (in shop)		1				
Install equipment — phase I			1	2	4	
Install equipment — phase II			1	2	4	
Develop operating procedures			2			
Select and train personnel			2			
Debug equipment			1	2	4	
Develop and design automatic controls			1			
Select controls supplier			1			
Fabricate and assemble controls package			1			

*DR, draftsman; D, designer; ENG, engineer; E, electrician; P, pipe fitter; L, laborer.

a. Find the total weekly requirements for each trade for the equipment installation project. (Use the earliest start.)

b. Level the labor within the present project duration.

c. Adjust the bar chart time schedule to reflect the labor leveling effort.

2. Repeat Problem 1 for the computer installation project.

Labor allocation

| | Workers per week | |
Job description	Analyst	Programmer
Decide on computer	2	—
Procure computer	1	—
Install and test computer	—	4
Determine site specifications	2	—
Solicit bids for site preparation	1	—
Award contract for site preparation	1	—
Prepare site	2	—
Select programming personnel	2	—
Select operating personnel	2	—
Train programming personnel	2	—
Train operating personnel	2	—
Layout computer records	—	2
Develop computer program	—	4
Test computer program	—	4
Design forms	—	2
Procure forms	—	2
Put program into operation	—	4

Index